GLOBALVIEWPOINTS

Women's Rights

Other Books of Related Interest:

At Issue Series

Beauty Pageants

Gay and Lesbian Families

Reproductive Technologies

Current Controversies Series

Human Trafficking

Global Viewpoints Series

Marriage

Population Growth

Introducing Issues with Opposing Viewpoints Series

Birth Control

Human Rights

Women's Rights

Issues on Trial

Abortion

Marriage

Opposing Viewpoints Series

Abortion

Civil Liberties

Male and Female Roles

Social Issues in Literature

Patriarchy in Sandra Cisneros's *The House on Mango Street*

GLOBALVIEWPOINTS

Women's Rights

Louise Hawker, Book Editor

GREENHAVEN PRESS
A part of Gale, Cengage Learning

GALE
CENGAGE Learning™

Detroit • New York • San Francisco • New Haven, Conn • Waterville, Maine • London

Christine Nasso, *Publisher*
Elizabeth Des Chenes, *Managing Editor*

© 2010 Greenhaven Press, a part of Gale, Cengage Learning

Gale and Greenhaven Press are registered trademarks used herein under license.

For more information, contact:
Greenhaven Press
27500 Drake Rd.
Farmington Hills, MI 48331-3535
Or you can visit our Internet site at gale.cengage.com

For product information and technology assistance, contact us at

Gale Customer Support, 1-800-877-4253
For permission to use material from this text or product, submit all requests online at www.cengage.com/permissions

Further permissions questions can be emailed to permissionrequest@cengage.com

Articles in Greenhaven Press anthologies are often edited for length to meet page requirements. In addition, original titles of these works are changed to clearly present the main thesis and to explicitly indicate the author's opinion. Every effort is made to ensure that Greenhaven Press accurately reflects the original intent of the authors. Every effort has been made to trace the owners of copyrighted material.

Cover image © Penny Tweedie/Corbis.

LIBRARY OF CONGRESS CATALOGING-IN-PUBLICATION DATA

Women's rights / Louise Hawker, book editor.
p. cm. -- (Global viewpoints)
Includes bibliographical references and index.
ISBN 978-0-7377-4474-3 (hardcover) -- ISBN 978-0-7377-4475-0 (pbk.)
1. Women's rights--Juvenile literature. 2. Women--Social conditions--Juvenile literature. I. Hawker, Louise.
HQ1236.W652652 2010
305.42--dc22
2010000084

Printed in the United States of America
1 2 3 4 5 6 7 14 13 12 11 10

Contents

Chapter 1: Women's Legal Rights

Europeans working in the sex industry, many of whom are migrants, are often denied their basic human and legal rights. Representatives from across Europe united to create an international committee that crafted a declaration of rights to which sex workers are entitled.

Chapter 2: Women's Reproductive Rights

Chapter 3: Women's Social Rights

Chapter 4: Women's Economic Rights

Foreword

*"The problems of all of humanity can
only be solved by all of humanity."*
—*Swiss author Friedrich Dürrenmatt*

Global interdependence has become an undeniable reality.
Mass media and technology have increased worldwide
access to information and created a society of global citizens.
Understanding and navigating this global community is a
challenge, requiring a high degree of information literacy and
a new level of learning sophistication.

Building on the success of its flagship series, *Opposing
Viewpoints*, Greenhaven Press has created the *Global Viewpoints* series to examine a broad range of current, often controversial topics of worldwide importance from a variety of
international perspectives. Providing students and other readers with the information they need to explore global connec-
tions and think critically about worldwide implications, each
Global Viewpoints volume offers a panoramic view of a topic
of widespread significance.

Drugs, famine, immigration—a broad, international treatment is essential to do justice to social, environmental, health,
and political issues such as these. Junior high, high school,
and early college students, as well as general readers, can all
use *Global Viewpoints* anthologies to discern the complexities
relating to each issue. Readers will be able to examine unique
national perspectives while, at the same time, appreciating the
interconnectedness that global priorities bring to all nations
and cultures.

Material in each volume is selected from a diverse range of
sources, including journals, magazines, newspapers, nonfiction
books, speeches, government documents, pamphlets, organiza-

tion newsletters, and position papers. *Global Viewpoints* is truly global, with material drawn primarily from international sources available in English and secondarily from U.S. sources with extensive international coverage.

Features of each volume in the *Global Viewpoints* series include:

- An **annotated table of contents** that provides a brief summary of each essay in the volume, including the name of the country or area covered in the essay.

- An **introduction** specific to the volume topic.

- A **world map** to help readers locate the countries or areas covered in the essays.

- For each viewpoint, an **introduction** that contains notes about the author and source of the viewpoint explains why material from the specific country is being presented, summarizes the main points of the viewpoint, and offers three **guided reading questions** to aid in understanding and comprehension.

- **For further discussion** questions that promote critical thinking by asking the reader to compare and contrast aspects of the viewpoints or draw conclusions about perspectives and arguments.

- A worldwide list of **organizations to contact** for readers seeking additional information.

- A **periodical bibliography** for each chapter and a **bibliography of books** on the volume topic to aid in further research.

- A comprehensive **subject index** to offer access to people, places, events, and subjects cited in the text, with the countries covered in the viewpoints highlighted.

Global Viewpoints is designed for a broad spectrum of readers who want to learn more about current events, history, political science, government, international relations, economics, environmental science, world cultures, and sociology—students doing research for class assignments or debates, teachers and faculty seeking to supplement course materials, and others wanting to understand current issues better. By presenting how people in various countries perceive the root causes, current consequences, and proposed solutions to worldwide challenges, *Global Viewpoints* volumes offer readers opportunities to enhance their global awareness and their knowledge of cultures worldwide.

Introduction

> *"We have to start looking at the world through women's eyes: How are human rights, peace and development defined from the perspective of the lives of women? It's also important to look at the world from the perspective of the lives of diverse women, because there is not [a] single women's view, any more than there is a single men's view."*
>
> *—Charlotte Bunch,*
> *American activist and a*
> *leading advocate for international*
> *human rights for women*

For those who live and work in countries such as the United States, the concept of women's rights has largely been defined by the political and social struggles of the last one hundred years. Those struggles have focused on issues such as the right to vote, reproductive freedom, and opportunities for career advancement. But in many other nations and cultures, women's rights advocates still focus on fundamental issues such as access to education, freedom from and within marriage, and combating legalized violence against women. Western readers cannot, therefore, apply their own template of cultural experience to achieving an understanding of women's rights in other parts of the world. What may seem, from a Western perspective, a small step forward for women in a different nation may actually be a significant and controversial change within that culture. So the term "women's rights" must be viewed in relative terms.

In early civilizations, women were often considered property, or chattel, subject to the dictates of a male relative or

14

husband. In ancient Rome, for example, women could not hold any position in public office, and were considered wards of their husbands. In early Athens, women had no rights in consenting to marriage. Islam granted many rights to women that were not yet accorded in other cultures. Between 610 and 661, Muslim women gained the right to consent to marriage, and their dowries remained as personal property after marriage. They also were awarded inheritance rights.

Women's suffrage, or the right to vote, provides a window into how legal rights have—or have not—been achieved around the world. For example, in 1851, Prussian law forbade women from joining political parties or even attending meetings where politics would be discussed. In 1869 Britain gave unmarried women defined as householders the right to vote in local elections. In 1880 the Isle of Man was the first country to give women the right to vote in national elections. By 1894 the United Kingdom had expanded voting rights to married women in local elections, but still excluded them from national elections. Many countries extended voting rights to women during the nineteenth century. Early in the twentieth century, the Nordic region nations gave women the right to vote. Starting in 1907, Norwegian women obtained the right to run for elective office. The 1917 overthrow of the Russian czar led to universal suffrage for women. Canadian women did not have the right to vote in most provinces until 1918— the same year that Germany and Austria adopted women's suffrage. For perspective, the amendment to the U.S. Constitution granting women full suffrage was adopted in 1920. Only white women were granted suffrage in South Africa in 1930; black women would not achieve full suffrage until 1994. Also in the 1930s, Turkey, Spain, Sri Lanka, and Bolivia were among the nations granting some degree of women's suffrage. The list of changes goes on, up to and including the 2005 granting of full suffrage to women in Kuwait.

Women's health and reproductive rights have endured a much stormier history, since reproductive rights are often subsumed by religious and cultural dictates. Access to abortion and family planning are often at the center of this debate. Women in countries heavily influenced by or subject to a state religion have been most affected by reproductive rights issues. As recently as 2003, Italy, a predominantly Roman Catholic country, passed legislation banning donor sperm, donor eggs, or surrogate mothers. Israel, in contrast, offers national health insurance that covers fertility treatment for all women, regardless of religious persuasion. In Kuwait married women have access to comprehensive health care and contraceptives through government health services, in spite of the belief by some that contraception violates Islamic law. In many nations, abortion is prohibited. According to the Center for Reproductive Rights, 26 percent of the world's population lives where abortion is generally prohibited; 61 percent live in countries where induced abortion is permitted to some degree.

Cultural values, including religion and a male patriarchy, have dictated a slow response to women's heath issues in Africa. Sub-Saharan African women have the world's worst statistics on women's health. The Protocol on the Rights of Women in Africa, passed in 2005, reaffirmed women's rights to reproductive choice. The protocol, however, was widely viewed as ineffective.

Women's religious rights have varied, with some liberalizing mandates issued that may be interpreted as restrictive by outsiders. According to IslamOnline.net, in Turkey the Religious Consultative Council issued a 2002 fatwa (an Islamic legal opinion or ruling) stating that wearing the hijab (a head covering worn by some Muslim women) is an inalienable religious right for women. The French Senate approved a bill banning the hijab in public schools in 2004.

Women as priests continues to be a controversial international issue in the Catholic Church. According to Women-priests.org, eight out of ten Catholic scholars in the world support ordination of women as priests. As recently as November 2009, the archbishop of Canterbury told the pope that the Catholic Church's refusal to ordain women is a bar to Christian unity.

Internationally, economic issues continue to limit the ability of women to support themselves and their families. According to *South-North Development Monitor* in March 2009, a report by the International Labour Office placed the global pay gap between men and women at 22 percent. The current global economic crisis is greatly impacting women's employment in Latin America and the Caribbean islands. In South Africa, land reform has not led to equal access for women, states Fazila Farouk in *Third World Resurgence*. Rural women, many of them single heads of households, often eke out a bare landless existence, despite apartheid reforms.

"Women's rights" will continue to be a relative term, subject to widely varying interpretations based on national and regional customs, history, and governmental policies. The selections that follow in *Global Viewpoints: Women's Rights* offer a starting point for examining this important topic.

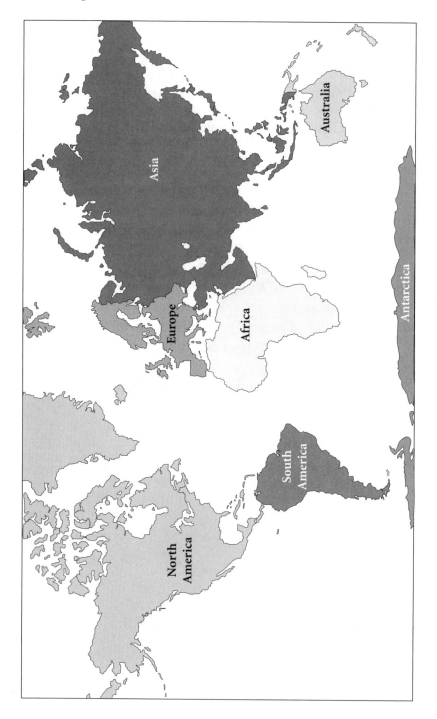

GLOBALVIEWPOINTS

Women's Legal Rights

South African Women Advocate Training for Women in Politics

Stephanie Nieuwoudt

The African National Congress (ANC) proposed that the number of women on its party lists be increased to 50 percent as a means of recruiting more women as candidates. As Stephanie Nieuwoudt reports in the following viewpoint, however, critics state that a quota system will not advance women's political positions since many are untrained and naïve about the political arena. The critics promote training and mentoring for women who wish to become involved in politics. As a woman official notes, women must fight for respect in local government since government "equal access" policies do not always filter down to the local level. Inter Press Service (IPS) is a global news agency headquartered in Rome, Italy, and is committed to offering a fresh perspective on development and globalization. Nieuwoudt is a journalist from the Cape Town area of South Africa.

As you read, consider the following questions:

1. According to the South African Local Government Association (SALGA) survey, what percentage of municipal councillors in South Africa have no idea about how financial structures work?

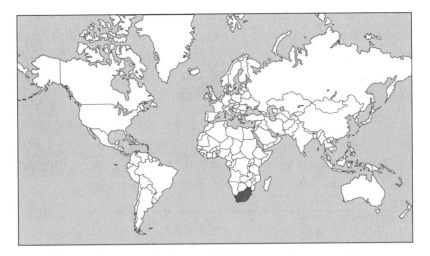

2. In what years was Eve Marthinus the mayor of Bredasdorp?

3. How many women does Stephanie Nieuwoudt assert
hold powerful positions in the Cape Town metropolis?

The African National Congress (ANC) directive to increase
the number of women on South Africa's ruling party's
election lists to 50 percent (up from 30 percent) might actually weaken the role of women in local government.

"The ANC took the 50 percent decision at its Polokwane
general meeting at the end of 2007. This does address the issue of gender equity, but it can also disempower women,"
Clive Keegan, director of the South African Local Government
Research Centre told IPS [Inter Press Service].

"If women are placed on a list simply to fulfil a quota,
there is a risk that the names of candidates without the necessary skills will be brought forward by men with their own
agenda. This means that some of these women will be easily
manipulated and susceptible to corruption. It could especially
be problematic in the poor areas where being a councillor is a
ticket out of poverty and where there is a huge skills shortage."

According to a recent survey by the South African Local Government Association (SALGA) one in three municipal councillors cannot read or write and more have no idea of how financial structures work. Thirty-two percent of these councillors need basic adult education and training.

"Without these skills they may never fully develop their abilities and optimally contribute to council activities—especially when affairs of council are driven by agendas, reports submitted and minutes," SALGA stated in its report.

"If women are placed on a list simply to fulfil a quota, there is a risk that the names of candidates without the necessary skills will be brought forward by men with their own agenda."

Attending Workshops Is Critical

Nomsa Bevu, a proportional representative of Sub Council 9 in the poverty-stricken township of Khayelitsha in Cape Town, says that she feels she has to work much harder than her male counterparts to prove herself.

"I make sure that I attend workshops and training courses so that I can do my job as well as possible."

Bevu says that during workshops she got to understand why it is necessary for people to pay for services like water. "Before I became a councillor I did not understand why one has to pay for water," she told IPS.

A number of courses about local government and the demands of specific portfolios are offered by SALGA and are well attended by members of all parties.

In the Kraaifontein area northeast of Cape Town, Buyiswa Blaai, an ANC sub-councillor, said that she has encountered building contractors and other business people trying to bribe councillors to give them contracts in housing developments.

African Women Gain Political Representation

At the recent Inter-Parliamentary Union (IPU) assembly, held during the first week of April [2009] in Addis Ababa [Ethiopia], Namibia was hailed as one of the seven African countries that has achieved more than 30 percent women representation in Parliament. . . .

Rwanda reinforced its position at the top of the scoreboard by electing more than 56 percent female members to its lower house, improving on its previous record set in 2003 of nearly 49 percent women members. Angola elected more than 37 percent women in its first election since 1992.

Michael Chebud, "Women Are Born Leaders,"
Inter Press Service, May 14, 2009.

"As women councillors and members of sub-councils, we have to be aware of these traps. In the end it is up to the individual, whether you are male or female, to be strong and resist corruption."

For many in the poor areas of the Western Cape, a job as a council member is a ticket out of poverty.

"Coupled with a desperation to hold on to a position that guarantees an income, and a severe skills shortage, it becomes easy for many to follow the corruption route," said Amanda Gouws, a political analyst at the University of Stellenbosch.

"When patron/client relations become part of the system, women and men of all parties are equally susceptible."

Some women in the ANC have risen to powerful positions in local government. One of them is Eve Marthinus who was the mayor of Bredasdorp in the Western Cape from 2006 to 2007.

"Many of the ANC male councillors have a lack of respect for woman and simply 'tolerate' us. They rule the caucus."

Women Must Fight for Respect

She is presently one of only three female councillors in her ward, which has a large constituency of extremely poor people. She says that she has experienced the negative side of men lobbying for positions in local government.

"Women in local government structures have to be extremely vigilant because we are seen as pliable. And when a person is pliable, it means that he or she can be easily corrupted," she says.

"The situation will only be redressed if more women make themselves available during elections and act in a forceful way. A quota system is not the answer if it is not supported by training and the appointment of strong women who know how to lead. If the women are not strong enough, they could become victims of patronage."

"Women in local government structures have to be extremely vigilant because we are seen as pliable."

Mercia Arendse, an ANC councillor from Mamre, a rural area on the Cape West Coast, says that she is fighting a continuous battle against men trying to fob off soft issues like food schemes and social issues on her.

"I do not believe that a women's agenda has to be pushed in council, but women are affected on different levels by many issues. If there is no service delivery such as water and power, women and children are the ones to suffer."

Policies Do Not Always Reach the Grassroots Level

Arendse says that the ANC is progressive in its policy of gender equality, which is empowering to women, but the rhetoric does not always filter down to grassroots level. "There are still too many men in leadership positions who continue to look at women in a patriarchal way."

Claire Mathonsi, women and governance project coordinator at the Gender Advocacy Programme in Cape Town, says "Not only are there gender struggles in the councils, but there are also faction struggles. Many women who serve as council members are co-opted. They carry on with the agendas that are already on the table and do not put forward new ideas."

Mathonsi adds: "The problem lies in the interpretation of what gender means and what needs to be done about the gender discourse. For the most part, equity has become a numerical thing. When a numerical target is met, it is wrongly believed that the issue of gender has been dealt with."

In the Cape Town metropolis, the Democratic Alliance (DA) has set a high standard with a number of powerful women. . . . Helen Zille is the mayor, Marian Nieuwoudt is the mayoral committee member on planning and housing, Anthea Serritslev is the chief whip of the city, Belinda Walker is in charge of corporate services and human resources and Elizabeth Thompson is in charge of transport.

"There are problems in all parties," Serritslev told IPS. "But once women manage to take on a leading role in their communities as council members, they, for the most part, seem to become strong. They are eager to fill up any gaps through training courses and workshops. Women councillors should encourage other woman to put their names forward during elections."

Bolivia Provides Technology to Support Female Indigenous Leaders

International Institute for Communication and Development (IICD)

Indigenous groups in Bolivia have been fighting for legal and other rights for more than three centuries, the International Institute for Communication and Development (IICD) describes in the following viewpoint. Indigenous women in Bolivia requested access to computer and information technology to further their abilities to participate in political processes and lobbying. A core group was trained, as IICD reports, with the intent to transfer their knowledge to a larger group. The project has yielded substantive results, with forty thousand indigenous people receiving information, according to the author, and Bolivian participants have been empowered to fight for their right to land titles and a stronger legal basis for their existence. IICD is a nonprofit foundation that creates practical and sustainable solutions using modern media and traditional media to connect people and enable them to benefit from information and communication technology (ICT).

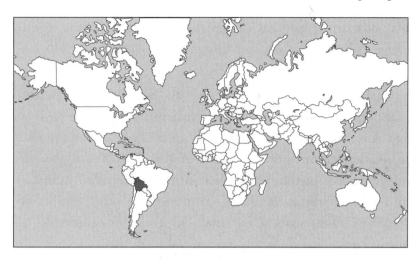

As you read, consider the following questions:

1. In what year did the Confederation of Indigenous People of Bolivia (CIDOB) begin using information and communication technologies, according to the author?

2. How many indigenous people does the IICD assert are using information and communication technology (ICT) on a regular basis?

3. What is one problem identified by the author?

For over three centuries, indigenous groups in Bolivia have been fighting for their legal, cultural, political and economic rights. As part of this, CIDOB [Confederation of Indigenous People of Bolivia] has been at the forefront of lobby activities through the organisation of large-scale national protests since the early 1980s. CIDOB still lobbies for the rights on political participation and original land rights and land use by indigenous people.

CIDOB has started in 2000 with the use of ICT [information and communication technology] to strengthen [its] political lobby by means of up-to-date databases and a Web site on legal land rights and use, and the building of ICT infra-

structure and capacities of the regional organisations to enhance communication and information within and between
the regional organisations.

Hitherto the project has generated awareness, empowerment and economic impact in terms of better access to land
and improved land-use planning. In total, 2,000 indigenous
people have been trained in basic ICT and 4,000 are now using ICT on a regular basis for communication and information on land rights, land use, institutional strengthening and
communication at local, national and international levels.

Increasing the Participation of Women

Since its start, IICD [International Institute for Communication and Development] and partners have been searching to
ensure the effective participation of women in ICT programmes. Over and over, the participation is hindered by
various practical obstacles, particularly related to the time-
bound limitations in the ability to participate in formal training sessions and follow-up use of ICT in daily operations due
to other responsibilities of women related to family and work
duties.

> *"Over and over, the participation [of women] is hin-
> dered by various practical obstacles."*

The objectives of the project are:

- A proactive and custom-made focus on building the
  capacities of ICT and related information and communication needs of women will assist in overcoming
  their limited participation in the use of ICT and, con-
  sequently, in the wider participation in leadership positions and decision making at both regional and na-

tional levels, even if not always present in all face-to-face meetings due to other responsibilities. Being able to manage ICT tools themselves, the core group will gain the capacities to have access to information and knowledge and to the means of communication required to participate effectively in decision-making processes.

• The use of a virtual closed platform for internal discussion among women leaders from the different regional organizations, who currently live scattered in distant geographic areas in the country. The platform provides an environment for exchange and discussion among peers. It specifically serves as a means of coordination in the preparation of political proposals by indigenous women.

• The chance to learn about the usefulness and impact of different ICT tools on the capacities and empowerment of women by setting up a program with three projects, each using different ICT tools.

Outcomes Have Been Impressive

Based on impact measurement among participants in the project, the impact has been very strong since the start in 2001:

• Satisfaction has been high according to 90% of the users;

• 70% of the participants indicate high levels of awareness and empowerment, mounting to 90% in 2007;

• The impact on transparency and political participation of the users has also increased sharply in 2007 with up to 85% of the users recognising a strong impact [of] this aspect.

Countries Whose Literacy Rate for Women Is Less Than 50 Percent That of Men

The better a woman's education, the better chance she and her children have of surviving economically, protecting themselves and leading healthy lives.

Country	Percent of Men's Literacy
Mali	49
Benin	49
Yemen	47
Mozambique	46
Ethiopia	46
Guinea	42
Niger	35
Chad	31
Afghanistan	28

"Ten Worst Countries for Women,"
womensphere, March 13, 2008.
http://womensphere.wordpress.com.

As for the more general impacts we can indicate in addition:

- The network has empowered the indigenous people in Bolivia in their fight for legitimization of land titles, the exploitation of these lands, and general development providing them with a stronger and legal basis of existence.

- The project has strengthened the organisation, communication, and information exchange between the dispersed indigenous people through the strengthening of the 8 regional indigenous organisations in Bolivia.

Using Experience to Plan for Improvements

- Indigenous people in general have been very eager to be trained in ICT as an instrument for political lobbying for land and other indigenous rights

- In particular, the young future indigenous leaders have benefited from ICT

- The strong impact on organisational strengthening at local and national levels has been an unexpected result of the project

- Notwithstanding limited financial capacity, the regional offices have shown to sustain ICT facilities in terms of finance and organization

- A particular problem is the fast change in leadership, requiring continuous training programmes for new incoming leaders

- A negative aspect women indicate [is] that they do not sufficiently benefit from the project due to cultural and physical barriers of entry to participation

Therefore, the project resulted in explicit demands from female indigenous leaders interested in gaining power in decision-making positions in the indigenous organisation. This demand has been honoured by the start of a new phase of the project focusing exclusively on female users.

What Is CIDOB?

CIDOB is a grassroots organisation of indigenous people in Eastern Bolivia, operating through 8 regional organisations and representing 34 indigenous people groups living in 1,500 communities with a total of 500,000 people in Bolivia. Thanks to the integration of ICT as part of their activities, CIDOB is now recognised as the indigenous organisation with [the] most experience in the effective use of ICT in Latin America.

Mexico Keeps Indigenous Women Out of the Political Realm

Diego Cevallos

In the viewpoint that follows, Diego Cevallos explains how indigenous women in Oaxaca called for the Mexican government to address their concerns, including a lack of services and infrastructure in their region. In September 2008, activists organized a march expected to draw ten thousand native women to Mexico City, says Cevallos, and government representatives promised to draw up a plan to address their concerns. In many villages, traditional customs result in subjugation of women's rights. Indigenous women, Cevallos asserts, are especially vulnerable to abuses, including not having the right to vote. IPS is a communications institution with a global news agency at its core, raising the voices of the South and civil society. Cevallos is a journalist who reports on issues affecting Mexico and Latin America.

As you read, consider the following questions:

1. How many native women held a protest march in Oaxaca, according to Diego Cevallos?
2. As Cevallos reports, what percentage of Oaxacans lives in rural villages of less than two thousand people?
3. What was the population of Mexico at the time this article was written?

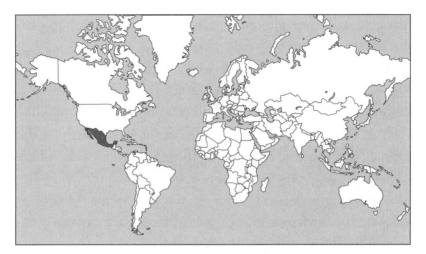

If the Mexican government has not addressed the demands of indigenous women in the southern state of Oaxaca by the end of the first week of September [2008], 10,000 native women will travel to the capital to directly pressure President Felipe Calderón. "We are fed up," said one of the leading activists.

Oaxaca Lacks Many Basic Services

"We have organised ourselves, and we are tired of being strung along and of being excluded," Leticia Huerta, an indigenous woman who leads the nongovernmental Coordinadora Estatal de los Pueblos de Oaxaca (State Coordinator of the Peoples of Oaxaca), told IPS [Inter Press Service]. Oaxaca is one of Mexico's poorest states and one of the districts with the highest proportion of indigenous people. Among the demands set forth by the native women, 5,000 of whom held a protest march Wednesday [in August 2008] in Oaxaca, the state capital, are the construction of a women's hospital in a rural area, medical posts throughout the region and the creation of an air ambulance service.

They are also calling for the construction of a bridge in a village that has been cut off for 12 years, a housing programme using local materials, and policies that would guarantee women's social and political rights.

Huerta said the Coordinadora has been working for women's rights for 17 years in Oaxaca, where 418 of the 570 municipalities are governed by indigenous "uses and customs."

The women's demands and the announced march to the capital "are the consequence of these years of work, which have raised our consciousness," she said.

According to Huerta, more than 10,000 women from 200 villages and towns in Oaxaca form part of her organisation, "which has no ties to any political party."

Delegates in Oaxaca from the governmental Commission for the Defence of Indigenous Peoples promised the women Wednesday that within the next 10 days they would draw up a plan to address their demands.

"We will make a 10-day halt in our activities, but we won't wait any longer than that, and if they fail to live up to their promise we will go to Mexico City in buses or any way we can, to demand a meeting with the president," said Huerta.

Nearly 60 percent of the population of Oaxaca lives in rural villages of less than 2,000 people.

In most of the villages, the local authorities are elected in traditional native community assemblies, without the participation of political parties.

In many of the villages, women are not allowed to seek public office, and under the local "uses and customs" many are not even able to study.

Traditional Customs Deny Women Rights

Studies by the National Women's Institute, a government agency, show that the sale of girls into marriage is a continued practice among indigenous communities in poor southern states like Oaxaca and the neighbouring Chiapas. Many young

Female Representation in Latin American Governments, 2006

The data represent the percentages of women elected to lower houses (LH) and upper houses (UH) of government in each country.

Mexico
22.6% LH
17.2% UH

Haiti
4% LH
13.3% UH

Dominican Republic
19.7% LH
6.3% UH

Nicaragua
15.2% LH

Costa Rica
38.6% LH

Columbia
8.4% LH
11.8% UH

Brazil
8.8% LH
14.8% UH

Peru
29.2% LH

TAKEN FROM: "Global Database of Quotas for Women," International Institute for Democracy and Electoral Assistance and Stockholm University, 2006. www.quotaproject.org.

girls are thus abruptly separated from their families, in exchange for a cash payment, or even just a crate of soft drinks or beer.

"Our rights are subjugated and the authorities and many men in our communities do not want to recognise them," said the activist. In November 2007, an indigenous accountant, Eufrosina Cruz, was not allowed to run for mayor of Santa María Quiegolani, a village of 800 Zapoteca people in the mountains of Oaxaca.

When she was nominated and voted for by some of the members of the all-male village assembly, the leaders of the assembly stopped the voting and tore up the ballots.

Cruz turned to the governmental National Human Rights Commission and received support from political parties and members of Congress, who called on Oaxaca state legislators to carry out legal reforms to ensure that traditional uses and customs were not used as a pretext for denying basic human rights guaranteed by the constitution.

"I'm not against uses and customs, only against abuses and customs. In this state there are 82 municipalities where women have no rights within their communities, and therefore they can't even express their opinions in assemblies, let alone vote or be voted for," she told IPS earlier this year [2008].

"Indigenous women are the most vulnerable group among the native peoples of Mexico, who are variously estimated to make up between 12 and 30 percent of the country's 104 million people."

Cruz was provided with police protection after she received death threats from men in her community.

Another case of violence against indigenous women in Oaxaca occurred in April [2008], when two young community radio station reporters, 22-year-old Felícitas Martínez and 24-year-old Teresa Bautista, were gunned down on a rural road.

In Oaxaca and Chiapas, the poverty level is similar to that of the Occupied Palestinian Territories, according to United Nations Development Programme (UNDP) studies.

In 2006, nongovernmental organisations and community groups in Oaxaca came together in a popular uprising against Governor Ulises Ruiz of the Institutional Revolutionary Party (PRI), which has governed the state since the 1920s.

The women represented by the Coordinadora Estatal de los Pueblos de Oaxaca have now presented their demands directly to the Calderón administration, because they have no confidence in Ruiz, who remains in his post despite numerous accusations of human rights violations, including murders.

Indigenous Women Are Particularly Vulnerable

Indigenous women are the most vulnerable group among the native peoples of Mexico, who are variously estimated to make up between 12 and 30 percent of the country's 104 million people. Their life expectancy is 71.5 years, compared to 76 years for indigenous men. Illiteracy stands at 32 percent among indigenous women, compared to 18 percent for men. And nearly 46 percent of indigenous women have not completed primary school, while a mere 8.9 percent have completed middle school (lower secondary school).

Costa Rican Women's Organizations Collaborate to Fight the Trade Agreement

Margaret Thompson and María Suárez

As reported in June 2007, Costa Rica was the only Central American country that had not ratified the Central America Free Trade Agreement (CAFTA). According to Margaret Thompson and María Suárez in the following viewpoint, women's organizations formed Women Against CAFTA to protest the act's expected impact on the national constitution that includes collective public ownership of basic utilities such as electricity and water. Activists feared CAFTA would privatize these utilities (known as the "commons") and this would lead to higher health and education costs and eliminate state jobs—especially those held by women. Women would be forced into lower-paying jobs with few benefits and no security, Thompson and Suárez contend. CAFTA was subsequently approved by national referendum at 51.6 percent yes, 48.4 percent no, in October 2007. Feminist International Radio Endeavour (FIRE) provides women with an international communications resource. Suárez is a Puerto Rican and Costa Rican feminist journalist and codirector of FIRE. Thompson is an associate professor of mass communications and journalism studies at the University of Denver. She has been affiliated with FIRE for ten years.

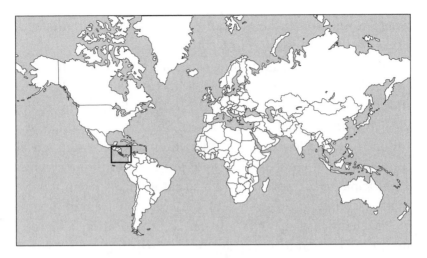

As you read, consider the following questions:

1. About how many years ago was the Tinoco dictatorship overthrown, according to the authors?

2. What percentage of the Costa Rican environment is protected, according to the viewpoint?

3. What is the name of Costa Rica's constitutional court?

Despite enormous pressure from the Costa Rican and US governments, Costa Rica is the only Central American country that has not ratified CAFTA—the Central America Free Trade Agreement [as of June 2007]. Heated debate and a growing social and popular grassroots movement, joined by former presidents, First Ladies, and former government officials in opposition to the treaty have resulted in a call for a public referendum in October of this year [2007]. Broad resistance to CAFTA in Costa Rica is also evident in recent public opinion polls.

FIRE [Feminist International Radio Endeavour] will be taking to the US Social Forum a Costa Rican women's initiative calling for solidarity in their resistance to CAFTA. The initiative will bring to the forum the "Quilt of Our Dreams" where women from the US can paint or write their messages of solidarity with women in Central America.

Women's organizations in Costa Rica have created the coalition "Women Against CAFTA" (Mujeres Contra el TLC) to mobilize for the *no* vote on the referendum. They reject CAFTA because of its impact in eroding the national Constitution [of Costa Rica], which is based on a social and political framework that emphasizes a state protector of human rights, a participatory democracy and a social services system involving the collective ownership of the commons (environment, water, electricity, airwaves and telecommunications). If ratified, CAFTA would override the Constitution and lead to privatization of the commons.

"Our country is an endangered species," stated María Suárez and Guadalupe Urbina of Costa Rica, when they visited the Global Fund for Women in San Francisco last February. "We need a population that is engaged to save it. Much of what has made Costa Rica a role model for democracy could be placed at risk because of the Central America Free Trade Agreement (CAFTA) and other economic policies."

"Much of what has made Costa Rica a role model for democracy could be placed at risk because of the Central America Free Trade Agreement (CAFTA)."

Sixty years ago, after a revolution to overthrow the dictatorship of [Federico] Tinoco [Granados], Costa Rica made the decision to dismantle the army. At that time, the leaders also created a social system dedicated to providing services for people and protecting human rights. In addition, Costa Rica safeguarded the "commons", which includes the environment (of which 60 percent is protected), and the notion that electricity, telecommunications and water belong to the society, and should not be privatized. Costa Rica developed a constitution and political process that established a space for people to work together to improve their nation. This is what has allowed the women's movement to achieve constitutional amendments that protect women's rights.

Privatization Impacts Women's Health and the Environment

Reports from *Estado de la Nación* (State of the Nation) and on Human Development from the UNDP ([United Nations] Development Programme) show women's growing impoverishment or "feminization of poverty" as a result of neoliberal policies, including those emphasized in CAFTA. The reasons for this are that women have always been the "poorest of the poor," but increased privatization has led to higher health and education costs, such that a growing number of families cannot afford proper medical care, nor to send their children to school. And it is the women who take on the extra tasks as substitute nurses, caretakers or teachers, often in addition to working at paid jobs.

Cuts in public spending have led to elimination of state jobs, particularly those held by women, and many end up in private sector service jobs with low pay, few benefits and no job security. Women are more likely to put themselves last, focusing more on their families when it comes to limited availability of food, education, and health care, and so are far more likely to be malnourished, illiterate, and have chronic health problems left untreated. In addition, declines in economic prosperity have contributed to a deterioration of social conditions, with widespread increases in crime and also violence, particularly against women.

CAFTA and neoliberal economic policies also have a devastating impact on the environment, with greater emphasis on agricultural expert production, which has provided jobs but has also led to greater pollution and environmental damage. Bananas, vegetables and flowers, and coffee production all require enormous amounts of fertilizer and pesticides, all of

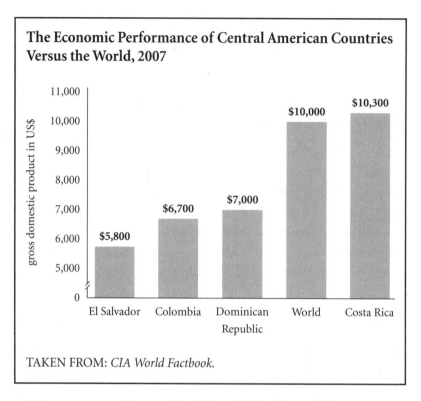

The Economic Performance of Central American Countries Versus the World, 2007

gross domestic product in US$

- El Salvador: $5,800
- Colombia: $6,700
- Dominican Republic: $7,000
- World: $10,000
- Costa Rica: $10,300

TAKEN FROM: *CIA World Factbook*.

which may contribute to health and fertility problems among workers and nearby residents, and particularly women.

> *"Women have always been the 'poorest of the poor,' but increased privatization has led to higher health and education costs."*

CAFTA Has Generated Widespread Opposition

CAFTA is a free trade agreement with the United States that, according to Eva Carazo Vargas, a trade and agricultural analyst with the International Relations Center (IRC) Americas Program, is "part of the [George W.] Bush administration's strategy to bilaterally impose a dependent free-trade regime, given its failure to achieve its objectives in multilateral forums such as the World Trade Organization [WTO] or the Free Trade Area of the Americas (FTAA)." But the negotiations were closed to the public, which has triggered demands for greater public involvement and dialogue as the Legislative Assembly debates a vote on whether to ratify CAFTA in order for it to take effect.

The struggle over CAFTA has generated an enormous grassroots social and popular movement with hundreds of forums and meetings organized to inform people and encourage dialogue and debate. Likewise, tens of thousands of people have joined street demonstrations in opposition to CAFTA, representing a wide diversity of groups such as the coalition of "Women Against CAFTA"; teachers; unions; indigenous, environmentalist, student, academic, religious and cultural groups; cooperatives; business; and politicians.

Opposition to CAFTA is growing, despite millions of dollars spent by the [Costa Rican president Óscar] Arias administration in ongoing media campaigns funded by large corporations and private pro-CAFTA foundation money, that include tactics ranging from promises of great economic benefits and half a million new jobs, to fear tactics about the commercial repercussions against Costa Rican industries and trade by the United States should the treaty be rejected. But according to Carazo, "The Free Trade [Area] of the Americas (FTAA) offers Costa Rica practically no additional benefit aside from those it already has in terms of trade with the United States, and a positive impact on employment has been belied by technical projected impact models."

CAFTA Is Subject to a Constitutional Challenge

The country is now awaiting the results of a constitutional challenge against CAFTA with the Sala IV (Constitutional Court), because the free trade agreement would override the Costa Rican Constitution in application of trade regulations.

A legal decision is expected in mid-July [2007]. In addition, the public will vote on the referendum on the treaty in October [2007]. [Editor's Note: CAFTA was approved by a close vote in October 2007.]

Opposition to CAFTA has also found its way in the US Congress, and [the] Democratic majority disagrees with some of its clauses also. Both Costa Rican and US citizens and opposing parties are calling for a total revision of the treaty under discussion, in order to guarantee protection of rights in both countries.

Europe's Sex Workers Sign a Declaration of Rights

European Conference on Sex Work, Human Rights, Labour and Migration

Sex workers in Europe, many of whom are migrants, are subjected to abuse and exploitation, often without any recourse, asserts the Declaration of the Rights of Sex Workers in Europe, drafted at the European Conference on Sex Work, Human Rights, Labour and Migration. This viewpoint contends that discriminatory legislation and tactics deny sex workers basic human rights under international law. One hundred and twenty sex workers and eighty allies from thirty countries came together to endorse the Declaration and raise awareness of sex workers' human rights. The Declaration cites a number of international treaties as its basis.

As you read, consider the following questions:

1. At the time the viewpoint was written, which countries had ratified the United Nations International Convention on the Protection of the Rights of All Migrant Workers and Members of Their Families?

2. In what month and year did Sexwork Initiative Group Netherlands (SIGN) SIGN ask sex workers across Europe to help plan a conference?

European Conference on Sex Work, Human Rights, Labour and Migration, *The Declaration of the Rights of Sex Workers in Europe*, Amsterdam, The Netherlands: European Conference on Sex Work, Human Rights, Labour and Migration, 2005. Reproduced by permission.

3. How many international treaties were referenced in drafting the Declaration?

D ifferent approaches have been adopted across Europe responding to the sex industry and female, male and transgender sex workers—including migrant sex workers—ranging from the acceptance of sex work as labour and the introduction of labour rights for sex workers through to the criminalisation of a wide range of practices associated with sex work, which at times results in the criminalisation of the status of sex worker, sex workers' partners or their clients.

Repressive Legislation Violates Human Rights

Over the last years [2003–05], legislative measures that restrict the fundamental rights and freedoms of sex workers proliferated at local, national and international levels, claiming to be in the interests of combating organised crime and promoting public health. However, many of these measures are implemented against the policy and principles set out by advice of UNAIDS [Joint United Nations Programme on HIV/AIDS] and the World Health Organization [WHO], which note that repressive legislation restricting the rights of sex workers in fact undermines public health policies by driving the sex industry underground, making practices central to safe sex evidence of crimes, such as possession of condoms. In addition, such measures contradict the European Parliament's Resolution on Violence Against Women that called for the decriminalisation of the exercise of the practice of prostitution, a guarantee that prostitutes enjoy the rights of other citizens, and the protection of prostitutes' independence, health and safety. Moreover, many measures are in violation of the obligation of states under international human rights law to respect, promote and protect the human rights of all persons within their territory, without discrimination, and including the right to privacy, to a family life, to legally leave and return to one's country, to be free from torture, inhuman or degrading treatment and from arbitrary detention, and in favour of the freedom of expression, information, association and movement.

Despite the fact that evidence shows that migrant workers in all sectors face increasing levels of abuse and exploitation with impunity, European responses to increasing international migration have focused on restrictive legislation with little attention paid to protecting migrants' rights and freedoms. To date, Bosnia and Turkey are the only European countries to have ratified the UN [United Nations] International Convention on the Protection of the Rights of All Migrant Workers and Members of Their Families, which came into force 1 July 2003.

Sex work projects and sex workers' organisations in Europe have substantial recorded and anecdotal evidence that discriminatory legislation and behaviour, which cannot be justified on the grounds of protecting public health or combating organised crime, restrict the fundamental rights and freedoms of sex workers, at local, national and international levels. These practices occur across health and social care, housing, employment, education, administrative law and criminal justice systems. Not all countries are listed below; however there is not one country within Europe—including those with regulated sex industries—where sex workers have not reported discrimination and violations of their human rights.

"There is not one country within Europe—including those with regulated sex industries—where sex workers have not reported discrimination and violations of their human rights."

Sex Workers Encounter Discrimination Throughout Europe

In Austria sex workers are subjected to mandatory sexual health controls, but other sexually active citizens are not, thus promoting the image of sex workers as 'unclean', and violating the principle of nondiscrimination.

In Finland, it is illegal for sex workers to work together for their own protection without the sex workers facing prosecution for 'pimping' one another, violating their rights to peaceful assembly and association and favourable conditions of work.

In France, a sex worker's child, upon reaching the age of majority, may be prosecuted with 'living off' the sex worker's earnings, violating the right of sex workers to respect for his/her private and family life and to be free from arbitrary interference with this right.

In Greece, where sex work is legal and sex workers [are] registered, a sex worker cannot marry. If they do, they are not allowed to continue to work legally and will lose their license. Sex workers are, therefore, forced to choose between the enjoyment of their right to marry and found a family *or* their right to livelihood and to practice a profession. No one should be forced to make this choice.

In Italy, with impunity, police confiscate and throw away or burn sex workers' possessions, thus violating sex workers' right to property and the state's obligation to provide an effective remedy in respect of protecting their right to property, to equal protection of the law and to protection against discrimination.

In the Netherlands, where sex work is accepted as legal work, migrant sex workers, as the *only* category of employees, are as a category excluded from getting legal work permits, thus violating the right to nondiscrimination; as for all other types of work, nonnationals can obtain a legal work permit when the conditions as laid out in the Law on Migrant Workers are fulfilled.

In Portugal (and many other countries) sex workers lose custody of their children through social services or family courts solely because of their occupation, and not based on any specific evidence of harm or incapacity to parent, violating their right to be free from arbitrary interference with their family life and nondiscrimination.

"In Sweden, politicians and policy makers have threatened to withdraw from public debates if sex workers are also to participate, and sex workers have been systematically excluded from public debate."

In Romania, where sex work is illegal, the government has forbidden its citizens to engage in sex work. As a result of pressure from the Romanian government, the Austrian government has terminated the permits of Romanian sex workers and women who have worked *legally* in Austria may face retribution on their return, violating their right to seek gainful employment in a country other than their own.

In Russia, police threaten sex workers that they will be sold into slavery and force them to have sex without payment, thus violating the obligation of the state to provide an effective remedy in respect of protecting sex workers' right to security of person and equal protection of the law.

In Slovakia, health care workers with impunity refuse medical care to sex workers and make discriminatory comments to pregnant sex workers challenging their suitability to bear children, violating their right to protection by the state of the highest attainable standard of physical and mental health and to found a family.

In Spain, sex workers in brothels are required to undergo and pay excessive fees for sexual health checks by the owners. The results of their tests are not treated confidentially; the state is failing to provide an effective remedy in respect of protecting their right to privacy, health and the violation of medical codes of practice.

In Sweden, politicians and policy makers have threatened to withdraw from public debates if sex workers are also to participate, and sex workers have been systematically excluded from public debate, violating their right to freedom of expression and opinion.

"There are, for sex workers in Europe, compelling reasons to avoid using the judicial system to challenge discrimination, violence, and other abuses through the courts."

In the United Kingdom, where street-based sex workers are criminalised, Anti-Social Behaviour Orders [ASBOs] are used to restrict freedom of movement and in some cities posters identifying sex workers with names and photographs have been printed and distributed in communities, violating the right to privacy and to participate in public life; exposing sex workers to discrimination and violence.

Under international law it is a fundamental human right that "all persons are equal before the law and are entitled without any discrimination to the equal protection of the law". However, there must be real doubt as to whether sex workers in Europe have, in practice, equal access to the protection of the law. There are, for sex workers in Europe, compelling reasons to avoid using the judicial system to challenge discrimination, violence, and other abuses through the courts.

This Declaration of Rights Was Initiated by Sex Workers and Activists

The process leading to the Declaration was initiated by SIGN (Sexwork Initiative Group Netherlands), a network of Dutch sex workers and sex worker rights activists. The establishment of SIGN was the first step toward creating a broader base of individuals from across Europe interested in organising a conference and advocating for the rights of sex workers in Europe. In June 2003 SIGN solicited participation from sex workers and sex worker organisations across Europe to join them in planning a conference. In January 2004 an international Organisation Committee (OC) was established consisting of 15 individuals, the majority being current or former sex workers, including migrants, from several European countries. The OC does not have representation from all countries or groups in Europe, but is supported by a large number of sex workers, sex workers rights activists and organisations working with sex workers across Europe and beyond.

It was decided by the OC that a Declaration of the Rights of Sex Workers in Europe would provide a framework for organising the conference and meet the ongoing need to raise awareness of sex workers' human rights and provide a framework within which to examine and challenge the undermining and violation of sex workers' rights.

The OC established a legal body, the International Committee on the Rights of Sex Workers in Europe (ICRSE) to both coordinate the conference and as a basis for future initiatives.

Although producing the Declaration was identified as the immediate task, the International Committee on the Rights of

Sex Worker Health and Rights Advocacy Groups Employ Web 2.0

Video and audio content is being created by a minority of [sex worker advocacy] groups who are publishing their work online on video-sharing Web sites such as YouTube and Blip. One organisation, COSWAS [Collective of Sex Workers and Supporters] (Taipei), is also producing audio podcasts. A few organisations are storing audio testimony privately as oral history, or to play at demonstrations and public events. Online photo albums are in use by some groups, such as COSWAS, who document their meetings with digital photos.

A prominent feature of the interviews with RedTraSex [Latin American and Caribbean sex worker network] in Buenos Aires and COSWAS was their interest in digital documentation. RedTraSex is using digital photography to document their demonstrations.... There was a lot of interest from the attendees in Cambodia in the possibilities of using digital photos for advocacy and aggregating them via photo-sharing Web sites like Flickr.

COSWAS is using digital audio to record the stories of sex workers.... These recordings are used as testimony in public hearings, as well as during actions, parades, and meetings....

APNSW [Asia Pacific Network of Sex Workers] has produced a karaoke video featuring a protest song used to promote a global advocacy message. This video was used as a public education piece at the XVI International AIDS Conference in Toronto [Canada], and is also being shared on YouTube and on Blip.

Tactical Technology Collective and Melissa Gira, "Sex Worker Health and Rights Advocates Use of Information and Communications Technologies Report," Open Society Intitute's Sexual Health and Rights Project, July 17, 2007. www.tacticaltech.org.

Sex Workers in Europe also committed itself to developing ongoing strategies for gaining public and political recognition and acceptance of the principles in the Declaration.

The Declaration Identifies Sex Worker Rights Under International Law

The Declaration is not intended to be a legal document and its existence does not establish a legal framework that protects the rights of sex workers in Europe. The Declaration merely identifies human, labour, and migrants' rights that sex workers should be entitled to under international law and points out the states' obligation to ensure:

- that it does not violate rights

- that others do not violate rights

- that all structures of the state are organised to ensure that diverse persons can enjoy and exercise their rights

The Declaration is a synthesis of all the rights that have been agreed in international treaties and covenants, to uphold for *all* citizens, together with specific proposals to states for steps and policies that would ensure the protection of those rights for sex workers.

The first section of the Declaration outlines the rights of all human beings within Europe. This is in all cases a simple statement taken from international agreements that European governments have signed.

The second section of the Declaration sets out measures for each of the identified rights that the signatories to this Declaration believe are needed to ensure that the rights of sex workers in Europe are respected and protected.

International Treaties Form the Basis for the Declaration of Rights

The international treaties that have been referred to in drafting this Declaration are:

1. UN International Covenant on Civil and Political Rights, 1966

2. UN International Covenant on Economic, Social and Cultural Rights, 1966

3. UN Convention on the Elimination of All Forms of Discrimination Against Women, 1979

4. UN International Convention on the Protection of the Rights of All Migrant Workers and Members of Their Families, 1990

5. UN Convention Relating to the Status of Refugees, 1951

6. ILO [International Labour Organization] Convention Concerning Forced or Compulsory Labour (no. 29), 1930 and the Abolition of Forced Labour Convention (no. 105), 1957

7. ILO Freedom of Association and Protection of the Right to Organise Convention (no. 87), 1948

8. ILO Migrant Workers (Supplementary Provisions) Convention (no. 143), 1975

9. European Convention for the Protection of Human Rights and Fundamental Freedoms, 1950

Moreover, it is based on a number of fundamental declarations:

10. UN Universal Declaration of Human Rights, 1948

11. UN Declaration on the Right and Responsibility of Individuals, 1999

12. UN Declaration on the Elimination of Violence Against Women, 1993

13. UN Declaration of Basic Principles of Justice for Victims of Crime and Abuse of Power, 1985

14. ILO Declaration on Fundamental Principles and Rights at Work, 1998

15. ILO ... Migrant Workers [Recommendation] (no. 151), 1975

16. European Social Charter, 1961 & 1996

17. EU [European Union] Charter of Fundamental Rights, 2000

The Declaration of Rights Specifies Threatened Freedoms

The International Committee on the Rights of Sex Workers in Europe selected from these treaties the rights threatened by discriminatory legislation and practice in Europe. They are:

- The right to life

- The right to liberty and security of person

- The right to be free from slavery, forced labour, and servitude

- The right to freedom from torture, inhumane, or degrading treatment

- The right to be protected against violence, physical injury, threats, and intimidation

- The right to privacy and protection of family life, including the right to be free from arbitrary or unlawful interference with privacy, family, home, or correspondence, and from attacks on honour and reputation

- The right to marry and found a family

- The right to liberty of movement and residence

- The right to leave any country, including one's own, and to return to own country

- The right to seek asylum and to non-refoulement

- The right to equal protection of the law and protection against discrimination and any incitement to discrimination

- The right to a fair trial

- The right to freedom of opinion and expression

- The right to work, to free choice of employment, and to just and favourable conditions of work and protection against unemployment

- The right to the highest attainable standard of physical and mental health

- The right to peaceful assembly and association with others

- The right to organise, to freedom of association, and to form and join a union

- The right to information for documented and undocumented migrants

- The right to an effective remedy

- Principle of nondiscrimination

- The right to participation in the cultural and public life of the society

- Obligation of states to combat prejudices and customary and all other practices which are based on the idea of the inferiority or superiority of either of the sexes or on stereotype roles for men and women

Within the Declaration itself we focus on those rights that are most threatened within Europe. The Declaration is not a demand for special rights to be given to sex workers, but is based on the principle that selling sexual services is not grounds for sex workers to be denied the fundamental rights to which all human beings are entitled under international law.

Burma's Military Regime Detains Political Activist Women

Marwaan Macan-Markar

Burma's military regime subjects both men and women opposition activists to long prison terms, claims Marwaan Macan-Markar in the following viewpoint. Burma's best-known political prisoner and Nobel Peace laureate, Aung San Suu Kyi, has been under house arrest for thirteen years. Female activists are treated harshly, Macan-Markar asserts, and some have even died in prison. Furthermore, secret trials are held inside prison walls with no opportunity for public scrutiny. International and United Nations calls to ensure human rights have gone unheeded by the Burmese government. Macan-Markar is a journalist at Inter Press Service (IPS) who reports on issues relevant to Asian nations. IPS is a communications institution with a global news agency at its core, raising the voices of the South and civil society.

As you read, consider the following questions:

1. What was the length of the jail sentence imposed on Win Mya Mya, as Marwaan Macan-Markar reports?
2. How many years has Aung San Suu Kyi been detained as of October 2008?

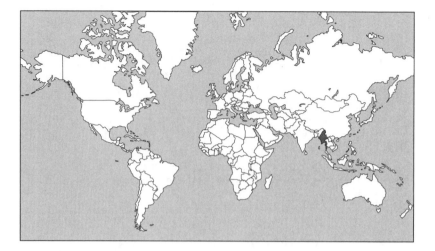

3. According to Macan-Markar, how many women disappeared during the September 2007 street protests?

When it comes to throwing pro-democracy activists in jail, Burma's military regime does not discriminate between the sexes. The junta treats women and men with equal measure of abuse.

The latest to be condemned to a long term in prison is Win Mya Mya, a woman in her 50s who served as a committee member of the opposition party, the National League for Democracy (NLD), in the central region of Mandalay. She was given a 12-year jail sentence on Friday [in October 2008] for her role in the September 2007 antigovernment protests led by thousands of Buddhist monks.

Five other leading NLD members from the same area—all men—were punished likewise, with jail terms ranging from eight to 13 years. They were accused of violating the laws 505 (B) and 153 (A), which makes it an offence to write, rumour, or report "by words, either spoken or written, or by signs" material that may "cause fear or alarm to the public," induce acts "against the state or against the public tranquility," or "promotes hatred between different classes (of persons)."

"Their trials were held in a court inside the Mandalay prison," says Bo Kyi, a cofounder of the Assistance Association for Political Prisoners (AAPP), a group championing the rights of Burmese political prisoners based along the Thai-Burma border. "The verdicts were also given inside that prison compound."

"The families of the accused were not permitted in the court when the verdict was given. The authorities didn't want the public inside the court."

It was a secret trial aimed to reduce public scrutiny, he added during a telephone interview. "The families of the accused were not permitted in the court when the verdict was given. The authorities didn't want the public inside the court."

International Pressure Has Been Ineffective

The date of this verdict could not have been more revealing. It confirmed how little the junta cares about international pressure against the harsh measures directed at political activists in Burma. October 24 [2008] marked 13 years that the country's pro-democracy leader and head of the NLD, Aung San Suu Kyi, has been detained.

There were multiple calls from governments in Europe and the United States and many regional and international human rights groups for the junta to free Suu Kyi, the country's most well-known political prisoner. The Nobel Peace laureate's current stretch of house arrest in the former capital of Rangoon began at the end of May 2003.

"As of Oct. 24, 2008, Aung San Suu Kyi has spent a total of 13 years under house arrest. We again call upon the Burmese regime to immediately and unconditionally release her and the more than 2,000 political prisoners it holds," said the U.S. State Department in a statement.

Suu Kyi and new political prisoners like Win Mya Mya are among the victims a UN [United Nations] human rights envoy for Burma had in mind when he told the UN General Assembly that the Southeast Asian nation has a system in dire need of reforms before the planned 2010 elections.

Tomas Ojea Quintana, an Argentine lawyer, called for changes in the system that has crippled political and civil liberties in Burma for decades. "These include revision of domestic laws to ensure their compliance with human rights; progressive release of all prisoners of conscience and reform of the military and independent judiciary," reports the *Irrawaddy*, a current affairs magazine published by Burmese journalists living in exile in Thailand.

"Burmese jails now hold 178 women prisoners of conscience, a threefold increase from the 53 imprisoned female political activists in August 2006."

Quintana's report to the General Assembly on Thursday [in 2008] was shaped by the information he gathered during his first visit to Burma in August. "The government didn't know me—it was difficult to go into prison," he is reported as having said according to the *Irrawaddy*.

But he did succeed in having three hours of "private meetings with detainees," adds the journal. "The prisoners were very open with me. It gave me a lot of sense of what was going on in the country," he said.

Burmese jails now hold 178 women prisoners of conscience, a threefold increase from the 53 imprisoned female political activists in August 2006.

Female Activists Are Treated Harshly

"During the [September 2007 antigovernment street protests] more than 157 women, including 10 nuns were detained. Nineteen women disappeared," reveals ALTSEAN-Burma [Al-

---

Number of Journalists Jailed Worldwide Continues to Rise

Countries with the highest number of imprisoned journalists as of December 2006:

1. China, with 31 imprisoned journalists
2. Cuba, 24
3. Eritrea, 23
4. Ethiopia, 18

America.gov,
"Number of Journalists Jailed Worldwide Continues to Rise,"
December 12, 2006. www.america.gov.

---

ternative ASEAN Network on Burma], a regional human rights body, in a note released this week [2008]. "Daw Ponnami, an 80-year-old nun at Thitsa Tharaphu monastery, partially paralysed by a stroke, was arrested and defrocked, accused of 'causing offence to the Buddhist religion', and remains incarcerated."

The other nuns who have been defrocked and jailed in this predominantly Buddhist country include 70-year-old Htay Yi and 64-year-old Pyinyar Theingi. The jails also hold such women as Su Su Nway, a 37-year-old labour rights activist, Nilar Thein, a 35-year-old university student leader, and Ein Khine Oo, a 24-year-old journalist.

Teenagers have not been spared either. In early August [2008], the regime arrested Ni Ni May Myint, a 19-year-old member of the NLD, and had her shackled. She and 50 others had gathered on a street in a town in the Arakan state, in western Burma, to pray for the students who had died during a brutal crackdown of the pro-democracy uprising in August 1988.

"I am worried about Ni Ni May Myint. The [prison] authorities will treat her harshly the way they treat other female activists in jail," says Khin Cho Myint, a 36-year-old former student of Rangoon University and a former political prisoner. "Women face a lot of verbal abuse and mental torture and it can be very frightening."

"There were times when women were kept in isolation and not given things they wanted for their health and sanitary needs," she added in an interview. "I faced this during the five years and nine months I was in prison. I was penalised for being a student activist."

But some female prisoners of conscience have faced worse, ALTSEAN-Burma reveals. "In August 2006, Nyunt Yin died in Insein Prison at the age of 60. She had served 16 years of a life sentence because of her involvement in the 1988 uprising. She was denied medical treatment for a heart condition."

Periodical Bibliography

The following articles have been selected to supplement the diverse views presented in this chapter.

Wajiha Al-Huweidar	"Covert Animosity and Open Discrimination Against Women Prevail in Arab Countries," Worldpress.org, November 3, 2006. www.world press.org.
Samia Allalou	"Algeria: Women's Movement Still Going Strong," Common Ground News Service, April 27, 2009. www.commongroundnews.org.
Burcu Bakir	"Does Europe Welcome Gay Politicians?" *New Europe*, November 1, 2009. www.neurope.eu.
Niusha Boghrati	"Iranian Police Attack Women's Rights Activists," Worldpress.org, March 28, 2006. www.worldpress.org.
Herizons	"Fewer Women Cast Votes in Afghanistan," Fall 2009.
Chelsea Jones	"Nepali Women Demand Equality," *Herizons*, Fall 2009.
Faiza Mardzoeki and Max Lane	"Indonesia: Fight Broadens Against Anti-Women Laws," *Green Left Weekly*, March 15, 2006.
Ron Moreau and Sami Yousafzai	"Information Blackout," *Newsweek*, August 21, 2009. www.newsweek.com.
Jill Moss	"Women Around the World Continue to Struggle for Their Rights," Voice of America, February 28, 2006. www.voanews.com.
Gila Svirsky	"The Peace Process Needs Women," *Israel Insider*, October 30, 2002. http://web.israelinsider.com.

GLOBAL VIEWPOINTS

CHAPTER 2

Women's Reproductive Rights

Indonesia Defines Reproductive Rights Within Islamic Law

Dewanti Lakhsmi Sari

According to Dewanti Lakhsmi Sari in the following viewpoint, the Koran gives women and men the same rights. In Indonesia, however, those rights are a mixed bag. Women are often treated as second-class citizens, she argues, especially in matters of reproductive health and rights. Most legal scholars of Islam agree that marriage is defined as a male's right over the female's body, however, Sari claims women have the right to decide the size of their family and on contraception. Abortion is also a complex issue in Islamic society and decisions generally do consider the danger of the pregnancy to the mother. Sari studied for a masters of comparative laws at the University of Delhi, India.

As you read, consider the following questions:

1. According to an international report, how many women die each year as a result of pregnancy or childbirth?

2. What does the Koran say about the condition of a pregnant woman in Dewanti Lakhsmi Sari's view?

3. According to the author, what do legal scholars of Islam say is the time limit after which abortion cannot take place?

Dewanti Lakhsmi Sari, "Women's Reproductive Rights in the Islamic Jurisprudence," The Indonesian Student Association in India, January 9, 2007. Reproduced by permission.

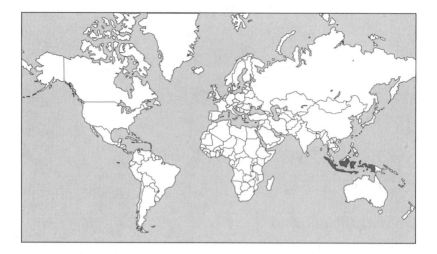

Islam exists to protect and free women from a life of torture. The Koran gives both females and males the same rights. Since the beginning, the Koran has had the intention of treating parents well, especially our mothers. The added emphasis of respect toward our mothers is a result of their experience of pregnancy and childbirth. This is similar to that mentioned in the Koran: "And we have enjoined on man (to be good) to his parents: in travail upon travail did his mother bear him, and in years twain was his weaning: (hear the command), Show gratitude to Me and to thy parents: to Me is (thy final) goal" (Luqman, 31:14). The verse above is associated with the reproductive health of women, which also forms a part of women's rights. As we all know women's rights are a part of human rights.

Women Are Treated as Second-Class Citizens

From here, we can see the importance in the need for discussion within the wider community of the problems associated with reproductive health and women's reproduction rights. Discussing issues like these, also means working on humanitarian problems. What is ironic is that there are many cases where women have not received the same rights, or are able to carry out the same behaviors, as those enjoyed by men. Women tend to still be pushed aside and considered second-class citizens to men. But, at the same time, they must carry out duties and support their households (husband and children). This fact can be witnessed everywhere, especially in villages and kampungs (traditional Indonesian village/quarter). Social events and activities are also evidence to the large number of cruelly treated women in Indonesia.

"On a social level, the position of women is generally not considered to be useful, while characteristics such as power and strength tend to be equated with males."

Violence against women continues to this day and is carried out everywhere, in a variety of ways including physical, mental and sexual violence. Situations of violence like these increase the seriousness and endanger the reproductive functions and bodies of females. An international report states that every year more than 500,000 women die as a result of pregnancy or childbirth, and 70,000 women die as a result of abortion or miscarriage. Seven million babies die every year as a result of the mother being physically unable or as a result of a shortage in obstetric checkups.... This data explain how very brittle the susceptibility of women's reproductive health is, and is thus closely intertwined with the reproductive rights of women. The core of all female problems is the struggle for women's rights, which at present is unequal. On a social level, the position of women is generally not considered to be useful, while characteristics such as power and strength tend to be equated with males (patriarchic). Now to look at the association between the reproductive rights of women and Islam, the author will try to explain the view of the holy Koran. This will be done methodologically with the use of fiqh [Islamic jurisprudence] using the comparison of interpretations by Islamic ulama [or ulema; legal scholars of Islam] and kaidah ushul fiqh [a rule proposal] in an attempt to consider the problems associated with female reproduction.

The Koran Seems to Give Men More Rights in Marriage

Human beings, aside from being intelligent creatures, are also sexual creatures. Sexual activity is a natural instinct of every human being. Within the teachings of Islam, all instincts of mankind are valued and respected. Sexual instinct should thus be channeled and not curbed. The curbing of one's instincts will increase negative effects, not only concerning a person's body, but also one's mind and soul. Marriage usually includes a sexual relationship. The definition of marriage varies in accordance with trends and the respective couples' view on it. Some people say that marriage is the unification of a male and female and validated by the law. In fiqh, the majority of fiqh experts define marriage as a male's right over the female's body for sexual enjoyment. Although the language can vary, there is an agreement among the majority of ulama that the covenant of marriage gives ownership to the male to obtain enjoyment from the body of his wife. This is because there is a general agreement that the male is the owner of sexual happiness. Islam exists to protect and free women from a life of torture. The Koran gives both females and males the same rights. Women have the right to treat men with nothing but goodness. We can thus use this view as a starting point, to formulate marriage as a legal promise, that gives both males and females equal sexual rights.

Based on equality and justice for both men and women, the problem of a sexual relationship can occur when the husband refuses to serve the sexual needs of his wife. Ibnu Abbas has said, "*I like to dress up for my wife just as she likes to dress*

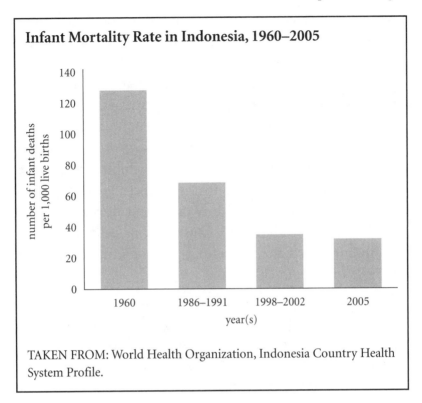

Infant Mortality Rate in Indonesia, 1960–2005

TAKEN FROM: World Health Organization, Indonesia Country Health System Profile.

up for me." This expression has the meaning that a husband and wife need to respectively give and receive, in a peaceful and loving atmosphere.

The Koran Says That Pregnant Women Are in a Condition of Weakness

Pregnancy on the one hand can form happiness for the wife, but on the other hand, it may also be something that has not been wished for. Aside from whether a pregnancy has been wished for or not, the Koran says that women who are pregnant are always in a condition of weakness. The level of weakness becomes greater at the time of childbirth. Professor Ida Bagus Gde Manuaba asserts that women experience many problems that can disrupt their health during pregnancy; among them are morning sickness, leg cramps, varicose veins, fainting, and leg swelling. It must be understood that child-birth forms a very critical point in a woman's life. Risks of fatality exist and can be caused by a variety of factors. The risks women undergo during pregnancy and childbirth can only be felt by women themselves, as [it] is only women who possess these reproductive organs. The two risks most commonly heard of are bleeding and miscarriage. How wise the Prophet was when he said: "There are seven possibilities to achieve martyrdom aside from dying in a war, these include, people that die as a result of poisoning, those that drown in water, those that fall ill with a virus, those that have leprosy, those that are burnt in a fire, those that are buried by scaffolding and those that die in childbirth." . . .

"The situation of maternal mortality places Indonesia as the highest-ranking country among countries of Southeast Asia, and fourth highest in the Asia Pacific."

The Prophet thus gives women who die in childbirth a guarantee into heaven. Their position in the face of God is the same as that of soldiers in fields of war, fighting against their enemies. The Prophet's statement mentioned above is no different from the high value placed upon women who die as a result of childbirth. But because many people still see dying a martyr as gaining a great amount of merit and the guarantee into heaven, those who are pregnant tend not to feel like they must give wholehearted care to their pregnancy. This is clearly a foolish idea. Results of expert research show that the position and reproductive health of women during pregnancy [are] very complicated, and thus childbirth is a primary killer of all fertile women. The situation of maternal mortality places Indonesia as the highest-ranking country among countries of Southeast Asia, and fourth highest in the Asia Pacific.

Women Have the Right to Decide the Size of Their Family

The increase in this problem means we need a deeper knowledge and a greater balance between men and women, so that women are able to reject pregnancy. What's more, women also have the right to make the decision of how many children they wish to have. No person can deny that inside the stomach of a pregnant woman is where a child grows and develops and while males do play a role in the fertilization process, it is the female who must experience the problems associated with childbirth.

There is a controversy concerning who has the right over the child. The majority of fiqh experts believe that children are the responsibility of both the father and the mother, as a child is the product of both parents. Because of this, to decide when to have children and how many children to have should become the right of the wife, but must be discussed by both parents. From here, we see the possibility to increase the decision-making capacity for wives and mothers, meaning their susceptibility to illness or maternal mortality at the time of pregnancy or childbirth, can be reduced.

The prevention of a woman becoming pregnant can be carried out in a number of ways and by use of a number of instruments, regulated by the family planning program. This can be by way of periodic prohibition or with other forms of contraception. With regards to the use of contraception, the wife has the right to decide what form of contraception she will use, in accordance with her health condition. It is thus logical that she also has the right to obtain information and an honest explanation from medical experts concerning her condition and choice of contraception. When she does not have any knowledge concerning contraception devices the doctor has an obligation.

Abortion Is a Complex Issue in Islamic Society

The use of contraception and other methods to prevent pregnancy cannot guarantee a woman that she will not fall pregnant. The choice for life (to become pregnant) or not, lies in the hands of God. An unwanted pregnancy (due to a variety of factors) can happen and these days happens on a regular basis. In regards to this situation then, can a woman cause a disruption/miscarriage to her pregnancy? As a principle, Islam prohibits, in all forms, the act of damaging, injuring or killing other human beings. The Prophet has said: "Do not cause damage (endanger) upon one's self or others." In a verse of the Koran a similar statement has also been made. Yet still in our lives we are faced with difficult choices. The issue of abortion is indeed one of these difficult choices.

To abort a fetus in the womb can mean killing a living spirit, but to neglect the continuation of life inside one's uterus for whatever reason, can result in suffering or, worse still, death to the mother. In regards to this problem, fiqh offers a number of choices. Firstly fiqh ulama agree that abortion cannot take place after the fetus is 120 days (4 months). A fetus that is 120 days old, in their view, is already a full human being. Many views concerning abortion of the fetus (before 120 days) do not consider this abortion, but murder. While on the contrary, Islamic experts hold a very pluralistic view concerning abortion, before the time mentioned above. Ulama concerning this issue base their view on al-Mukminun verse 12–14:

> Man we did create from a quintessence (of clay); Then we placed him as (a drop) sperm in a place of rest, firmly fixed; then We made the sperm into a clot of congealed blood; then of that clot we made a (fetus) lump; then We made out of that lump bones and clothed the bones with flesh; then We developed out of it another creature. So blessed be God, the Best to Create!

This verse positions the formation of mankind into three categories: nutfah, alaqah, and mudghah.

A more lax stance on this issue has been put forward by al Hashkafi bermazhab Hanafi. Abortion, in his opinion, can be carried out before 120 days, whether there is a valid reason or not. Al Karabisi from Mazhab Syafi'i, like that noted by al-Ramli in Nihayah al-Muhtaj, only agrees with abortion when it is still in the shape of when the sperm first meets the egg (before fetus has begun to develop). A more strict view can be found by al-Ghazali from Mazhab Syafi'i. He forbids abortion from the time of fertilization. This opinion is also that of the majority of Mazhab Maliki followers (school of thought concerning Islamic law), ibnu Hazm al Zhahiri and a portion of Syi'ah.

"All of the prior constructed thinking, concepts, and rules in life should be formulated by the Muslim community intelligently and then applied and monitored to their respective social lives."

Abortion Decisions Consider Dangers to the Mother

For as long as abortion has been investigated through fiqh literature, there tends to be an agreement on behalf of the ulama, without looking at the age of the fetus, that abortion can be carried out if the fetus during pregnancy endangers or threatens the life of the mother, and of course that this also has been assured by a doctor or medical expert. This view shows that the safety of the mother is put in front of the safety of the unborn fetus. Fiqh views the death of the fetus as a smaller risk than that of the death of the mother, because the mother is the originator of the baby or fetus; the mother is already in existence. The mother also has a number of obligations. While the fetus or baby is inside the womb, although it does already exist, it does not represent an obligation to other humans "so if a dilemma occurs, it (the fetus/unborn baby) is considered the victim with the smaller risks."

The view of the fiqh experts above concerning the motives of abortion appears to be limited by health and medical indicators. Other motives like social indicators including economic, political and psychological have not yet been given an extensive explanation. But it is interesting when we monitor that ulama from the Mazhab Hanafi [an Islamic legal school] train of thought allow abortion without requiring any specific reasoning. Finally, one issue that needs to be emphasized in the relationship between humans is the importance of a relationship based upon gender equality. Islam is a just religion, a religion that rejects all forms of discrimination and all forms of violence. We are born to build and uphold the supreme principles of mankind. All of the prior constructed thinking, concepts, and rules in life should be formulated by the Muslim community intelligently and then applied and monitored to their respective social lives.

Denmark Promotes Equity in Sexual and Reproductive Health and Rights

Royal Danish Ministry of Foreign Affairs

As stated by the Royal Danish Ministry of Foreign Affairs in the viewpoint that follows, sexual and reproductive health and rights are to be respected and protected by the state. Denmark places a high value on promoting these rights and meeting international commitments set out by the United Nations. Sexual and reproductive health and rights are keys to gender equality. Achieving gender equality internationally, however, requires changes to the power structure, an important criterion if Denmark is to deliver development assistance to other nations. The Royal Danish Ministry of Foreign Affairs manages foreign affairs and relations for Denmark.

As you read, consider the following questions:

1. What region of the world is a special focus for Danish development assistance in combating HIV/AIDS?

2. According to the Danish government, what are the three entry points to working with gender equality?

3. As defined by the Danish International Development Agency (DANIDA), to what age group do the terms "youth" and "young people" refer?

Royal Danish Ministry of Foreign Affairs, "Section 3, Promoting Social Development," *The Promotion of Sexual and Reproductive Health and Rights—Strategy for Denmark's Support,* May 2006, pp. 4–7. Copyright © 2006 Ministry of Foreign Affairs. Reproduced by permission.

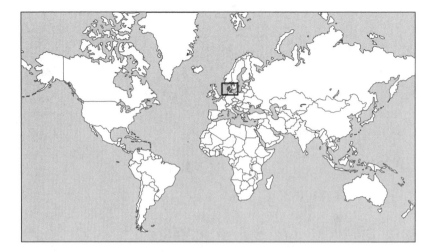

Danish efforts within the field of sexual and reproductive health are based on a rights-based approach where participation, inclusion and accountability are central principles. This approach views citizens not as passive receivers of services or beneficiaries of programmes but as active rights holders, who should be empowered to claim their rights. States have obligations to respect these rights and protect their citizens against violations. Fulfilling the right to sexual and reproductive health will require the building of responsive, equitable health, education and legal systems, as well as addressing underlying determinants of SRH [sexual and reproductive health]. It implies that states, policy makers and others are accountable to their people. It is recognised that fulfilling these rights will require time, money, commitment and action.

Reproductive rights embrace certain human rights that are already recognised in national laws, international human rights documents and other relevant United Nations documents. These rights rest on the basic right of all couples and individuals to decide freely and responsibly the number, spacing and timing of their children and to have the information and means to do so, and the right to attain the highest standard of sexual and reproductive health. It also includes their right to make decisions concerning reproduction free of discrimination, coercion and violence, as expressed in human rights documents. . . . The rights-based approach was reaffirmed and extended by the Fourth [World] Conference on Women in Beijing in 1995: "Human rights of women include their right to have control over and decide freely and responsibly on matters related to their sexuality. . . ." This paragraph is regarded as setting forth a definition of sexual rights. . . .

International Legal Framework:

1. Universal Declaration of Human Rights 1948

2. The International Covenant on Economic, Social and Cultural Rights 1976

3. The Convention on the Elimination of All Forms of Discrimination Against Women 1979

4. The Convention on the Rights of the Child 1989

Denmark Actively Promotes Sexual and Reproductive Health

Promoting sexual and reproductive health and rights has high priority in Danish development assistance. It is an integral part of Danish multilateral and bilateral policy dialogue and support. Denmark considers it an important—and necessary—task to actively promote, defend and protect these rights.

It is crucial for Denmark that the international commitments made and goals and targets set in the twenty-year Programme of Action . . . and at the Special Session of the United Nations General Assembly in 1999 . . . as well as in the Beijing [Declaration and] Platform for Action (1995) are not evaded, renounced or weakened. Danish policy, support and cooperation within the field of population are based on these documents. There have been many attempts to undermine international commitments since 1994, and it is foreseen that also in coming years there will be a continuous need to ensure that the Cairo agenda [United Nations International Conference on Population and Development, Cairo, 1994], and the principles and rights it stands for, is actively confirmed and promoted as a central and necessary element in fighting poverty and achieving the MDGs [United Nations Millennium Development Goals].

Denmark deliberately uses the term "sexual" together with reproductive to underline that sexuality and the purpose of sexual activity/relations is not limited to reproduction. It also includes the recognition of homosexuality. This approach is rooted in the belief that sexual health care and human sexuality also contribute to the quality of life and well-being—both mentally and physically—and enhance personal relations.

Denmark is convinced that women should have access to safe and legal abortion and postabortion care. Without access to safe and legal abortion, women are not fully able to decide freely on matters related to their sexual and reproductive health and, thus, not able to fully enjoy their human rights. Abortion should not be promoted as a method of family planning. Denmark believes that the best way to avoid abortions is through improved access to reproductive health services (contraception) and information, and the empowerment of women.

"Without access to safe and legal abortion, women are not fully able to decide freely on matters related to their sexual and reproductive health and, thus, not able to fully enjoy their human rights."

Denmark Uses an Integral Approach

In accordance with the Cairo agenda, sexual and reproductive health and rights are promoted through an integrated approach. Sexual and reproductive health is affected by the socioeconomic, cultural and political environment, and related to individual and collective rights and responsibilities. Sexual and reproductive health and rights are closely interlinked with promoting gender equality and fighting HIV/AIDS. Increased understanding and acceptance of this will serve to improve synergies and impact both in international development cooperation and at country level.

Danish efforts will involve broader development interventions through a number of sectors that impact women and adolescent girls' health—not least education of girls. The health sector, however, is the prime provider of the essential sexual and reproductive health services. It is essential that the sector has the capacity to meet the peoples' needs qualitatively and quantitatively, especially with respect to gender and protection against coercion and discrimination. Health staff have a proactive role in informing users about their rights and options in relation to reproductive health, fertility regulation, sexual abuse, and violence, all of which are human rights issues.

Combating HIV/AIDS is a strategic priority for Danish development assistance, with a special focus on sub-Saharan Africa. The HIV/AIDS strategy of April 2005 aims to strengthen and focus Denmark's contribution toward reaching the internationally agreed HIV/AIDS targets through its multilateral and bilateral development cooperation. Denmark supports the development of comprehensive global and national strategies that address HIV/AIDS in a balanced way, integrating prevention, care and treatment interventions. Priority areas of intervention include addressing the specific needs of women and girls, adolescents and other young people, children and orphans and people in conflict situations. Integrating sexual and reproductive health and HIV/AIDS efforts, and fighting stigma and discrimination are other priorities. . . .

Gender equality is a key crosscutting issue in Danish development assistance. The strategy on gender equality in Danish development assistance highlights three overall entry points to working with gender equality: promotion of equal rights, women's access to and control of resources, and equal political

Denmark's Share of the HIV-Positive Population, 2007

Indicator	Year	Denmark	Western Europe	World
Adults and children living with HIV	2007	4,800	730,000	33,000,000
Adults (ages 15+) living with HIV	2007	4,800	730,000	30,800,000
Women (ages 15+) living with HIV	2007	1,100	200,000	15,500,000
Children (ages 0–14) living with HIV	2007	No data	1,300	2,000,000
AIDS orphans currently living (ages 0–17)	2007	No data	No data	15,000,000
Adults and child AIDS deaths	2007	No data	8,000	2,000,000

TAKEN FROM: UNAIDS, 2008.

and economic influence. Gender equality—in terms of equal rights, including sexual and reproductive rights, equal access to and control over resources and equal opportunities to achieve political and economic influence—is central for women to become fully integrated and equal citizens in their countries and thus to fulfil their enormous potential for contributing to and benefiting from the development of their countries. The fulfilment of the potential of women has important implications for efforts to reduce poverty and promote economic growth.

> *"Danish efforts in the field of gender equality focus in particular on violence against women during peacetime and situations of armed conflicts, sexual and reproductive rights in relation to health, HIV/AIDS, and access to resources."*

Empowerment is a key condition for enabling women to demand and make use of equal rights, resources, and influence and thus for gender equality. The concept implies that each individual acquires the ability to think and to act freely, to make decisions and to fulfil his or her own potential as a full and equal member of society. . . .

Gender Equality Requires Changes to the Power Structure

Internationally, Danish efforts in the field of gender equality focus in particular on violence against women during peacetime and situations of armed conflicts, sexual and reproductive rights in relation to health, HIV/AIDS, and access to resources. The strategy emphasises mainstreaming of gender equality in sector support and in national Poverty Reduction Strategies, and in the support for human rights, democratisation and good governance.

Promoting gender equality demands changes to existing power structures together with the status and role of women and men. Therefore, it must be based on acknowledgements of cultural and religious differences within the frames of universal human rights. However, religious and cultural values and traditions must never be allowed to serve as an excuse for depriving the individual—woman or man—of her/his freedom and rights.

Men's responsibility for supporting women's SRHR [sexual and reproductive health rights] is vast—as a decision maker, father, husband, lover, brother, and son. Men's participation in improving women's SRHR is far more important than previous policies have reflected. Traditional norms for masculinity are often embedded in heterosexuality together with power over and dominance of women. Part of the mainstreaming of gender equality is therefore questioning the traditional norms for both sexes to give way to a broader and more varied set of roles for men and women.

Violence against women, family planning, prevention of STI [sexual transmitted infection] and respecting women's rights are all related to how men and women interact. Women's SRHR are highly related to the prevailing perceptions of women's roles and rights in society and in the family: the more gender inequalities, the poorer the SRHR of women.

"Religious and cultural values and traditions must never be allowed to serve as an excuse for depriving the individual—woman or man—of her/his freedom and rights."

Educating Girls Is Key to Their Reproductive Health

It is well documented that girls' education is a key instrument for empowering girls and women and for improving their SRHR, including the prevention of HIV/AIDS. Being in schools, even in schools of poor quality, is protective from a reproductive health standpoint—delaying sexual initiation, increasing chances of condom use, and decreasing forced sex. . . .

At the same time, education is an opportunity to teach adolescents girls and boys life skills including population, reproductive psychology, and physiology issues. Denmark promotes life skills education as part of the standard national teaching curricula for pupils and teachers. Danish efforts to promote girls' education are based on Education for All— Dakar Framework for Action and the United Nations Girls' [Education] Initiative.

Denmark Works to Protect Children's Health Rights

To further develop its assistance to children and young people, DANIDA [Danish International Development Agency] has developed guidelines to secure inclusion of children and young people in the various sector programmes, when appropriate. They list the main priorities, structured according to the Millennium Development Goals—six of the MDGs refer specifically to children, as they point to safeguarding the rights of children to health, education, protection and equality—and provide a course of action for follow-up and review. The guidelines also include a chapter about children and young people in crisis, conflict and injustice. These situations make children and young people more vulnerable to sexual violations and unsafe sex.

In accordance with the DANIDA guidelines, the terms youth and young people will be used for persons aged 10–24.

Peru's Conservative Political Leaders Impede Progress on Reproductive Rights

Anna-Britt Coe

In the following viewpoint, Anna-Britt Coe claims that Peru's conservative government has been the chief obstacle to achieving reproductive rights for women. Stakeholders identified five priority problem areas including unsafe childbirth and abortion, unwanted pregnancy, HIV and other sexually transmitted diseases, cervical cancer, and gender-based violence. At the time this viewpoint was written, Peruvian president Alejandro Toledo was acting on pressure to back family planning policies and replace ultraconservative cabinet members who did not support reproductive health and rights. Reproductive Health Matters publishes journals and books that provide coverage of sexual and reproductive health and rights issues. Coe, a sociologist, is a doctoral candidate at Umeå University, Sweden. She previously worked for the U.S.-based Center for Health and Gender Equity (CHANGE).

As you read, consider the following questions:

1. What is the change in the number of women infected with HIV from a decade ago, in Anna-Britt Coe's estimation?

2. According to a study, what percentage of women in Lima reported having been physically and/or sexually abused by an intimate partner?

3. In what year was emergency contraception approved in Peru?

Abstract: This article examines Peru's population policy since the 1994 International Conference on Population and Development and assesses to what extent its policies and programmes have affected reproductive health and rights. It is drawn from data collected during ongoing monitoring of sexual and reproductive health policies and programmes in Peru since 1998 for the Center for Health and Gender Equity (CHANGE). Accomplishments since 1994 in Peru demonstrate good faith on the part of the government and foreign donors to make progress towards fulfilling the ICPD agenda by addressing key reproductive health concerns and promoting women's rights. Unfortunately, this progress has not been consistent. It has been overshadowed by two periods of anti-choice policies and interventions. The first, in 1996–97 under the Fujimori government, was a demographic approach that used numerical targets and undue pressure on women to accept sterilisation as the government's main poverty reduction strategy, which led to documented abuses. The second, in 2001–03 under the Toledo government, was a far-right approach that worked to limit access to essential services, including emergency contraception, condoms and post-abortion care. In spite of their contradictory nature, these two policy approaches have been the greatest obstacles to making long-lasting improvements to reproductive health and rights in Peru.

For women's health advocates, the consensus forged at the 1994 International Conference on Population and Development (ICPD) was the result of decades of hard work to shift the focus of population policies away from the fulfilment of demographic goals toward the promotion of reproductive health and rights. However, participants faced their greatest challenge when they returned to their home countries—ensuring that governments adopted and met the goals set forth in the new agenda. Concretely, governments must replace narrowly defined fertility reduction strategies with broader policies that work to enhance women's and men's capacity to exercise their rights and address their reproductive health concerns, including but not limited to their need for contraceptives. This has proven to be far more difficult than expected, in part because many governments have limited technical and financial capacity to make and sustain the necessary changes. These changes also imply a long, slow process of transforming unwieldy bureaucratic structures and programmes.

However, the greatest obstacles to promoting the ICPD Programme of Action are policy positions that are frankly opposed to reproductive rights. These political positions may prevent governments from making a full-fledged commitment to achieving reproductive health and rights objectives. Peru is a telling example of the complexities involved in developing a reproductive health and rights agenda. Until the early 1990s, the government gave little support to population issues and its public family planning programme was poorly organised and relatively ineffective.[1-3] Since signing the ICPD agreement, the Peruvian government has taken several steps toward fulfilling reproductive health and rights objectives.[3-5] Progress has been overshadowed, however, by two periods of adverse policy approaches—demographic (1996–1997) and far right (2001–2003).[6-9] This article examines Peru's population policy since the ICPD and assesses to what extent the policies and measures adopted have enhanced or detracted from reproductive health and rights.

Methodology

The data are drawn from the author's ongoing monitoring of sexual and reproductive health policies and programmes in Peru since 1998 for the Center for Health and Gender Equity (CHANGE). The purpose of this monitoring has been to assess Peru's progress in implementing a reproductive health and rights agenda, including commitments agreed at ICPD, and the use and effectiveness of US foreign assistance in meeting this goal. It has consisted of two phases.

During the first phase, primary and secondary data were collected from key national-level stakeholders in reproductive health policies: women's rights groups, reproductive health NGOs, government institutions and international donor and technical assistance agencies. A total of 45 in-depth interviews were carried out with stakeholder representatives in April–June 1998 and October–December 2000 (Table 1 [not shown]). In-depth interviews were semi-structured using a topic guide with open-ended questions. Key informant interviews were designed to follow up on the same topics. Participant observation was used at public conferences, workshops and presentations organised by key stakeholders, and involving policy makers, programme directors and health care providers. Direct observations were made of service delivery in on-site visits in Ayacucho Department. Official documents and research studies produced by key stakeholders were reviewed.

Information was sought on the following issues:

- What are the priority reproductive health issues faced by women?

- How do the government and key international donors define population policy in Peru?

- What are the formal policies regarding population issues, family planning and contraceptive delivery, STIs and HIV, maternal mortality, cervical cancer and reproductive rights?

- What steps have been taken to develop policies that promote reproductive health and rights in Peru? What is the relationship between demographic goals and contraceptive delivery, including targets, fertility reduction and rhetoric vs. practice?

- What has been accomplished and what have the constraints been?

- What are the main issues concerning health services, including method mix, provider biases, use of integrated and innovative approaches, education and counselling, prevention and treatment, private vs. public sector services?

- What more is needed to improve the promotion of reproductive health and rights in Peru?

Data were processed, categorised and analysed by the author. Hand-written notes of observations and interviews were entered into a computer word-processing programme. Preliminary codes were given to the data at this stage based on the main themes and topics identified in the information. The data were analysed soon thereafter and preliminary codes were revised into first-level codes. Once first-level codes were assigned, the data were retrieved and sorted using the "find" key in the word-processing programme. A separate word-processing file was created for each main topic that emerged from retrieving and sorting the data according to first-level codes. Data in each file were analysed to identify patterns within the particular theme of the first-level codes. Patterns were given second-level codes and sorted using the "find" key in the word-processing programme. A separate word-processing file was created for each pattern that was identified through the second-level codes. Information and interview transcripts from different points in time were compared for continuity and change. The author presented the data in two internal reports, July 1998 and in July 2001.

During the second phase, since 2001, I have participated on behalf of CHANGE in a coalition of civil society organisations in Peru, *Mesa de Vigilancia de Derechos Sexuales y Reproductivos* (Monitoring Group on Sexual and reproductive Rights). This entity regularly shares and collectively analyses policy information and events on sexual and reproductive health in order to develop appropriate advocacy responses. Simultaneously, I have documented the alliance between far right actors in Peru and the US, and their assault on reproductive health programmes funded by the US government in Peru, through information obtained from key informants, the Web pages of far right organisations and internal, confidential documents.

Key Priorities for Women's Health in Peru

All key stakeholders repeatedly pointed to five priority sexual and reproductive health problems in Peru, backed by quantitative and qualitative data:

- unsafe childbirth and abortion

- unwanted pregnancy

- STIs/HIV

- cervical cancer

- gender-based violence.

The maternal mortality ratio, currently estimated at 185 deaths per 100,000 live births, is very high for the region, according to the Pan American Health Organization. Additionally, the national average masks the reality of far higher numbers of maternal deaths in rural and peri-urban areas, and in certain Andean and Amazonian departments. Unsafe abortion accounts for an estimated 16% of pregnancy-related deaths.[9] Approximately 66 abortions occur for every 100 live births in Peru, where abortion is illegal and safe abortions rare.[10] At least 30% of all abortions result in complications.[11]

"The maternal mortality ratio, currently estimated at 185 deaths per 100,000 live births, is very high for the region."

In Peru, 60% of all pregnancies are unwanted, and an estimated 25% of all sexually active women of reproductive age in Peru are not adequately protected against an unwanted pregnancy.[11] Despite consistent increases over the last decade in contraceptive prevalence rates, access to quality information and services varies widely according to socio-economic status, age group and place of residence.[12] Adolescent girls are particularly vulnerable as they have the least access to contraceptive methods. Although there are insufficient data available to present a complete picture of the magnitude of STIs, including HIV, evidence shows that women are increasingly at risk of infection.[13] A decade ago, women accounted for one out of 15 people infected with HIV; currently, they make up one in three.[14] Women of reproductive age are most likely to die of cancer, and 48% of these deaths are due to a gynaecological cancer, mainly cervical or breast cancer.[15]

Indigenous Peruvian Women Are Often Denied Reproductive Health Care

Hundreds of poor, rural and indigenous pregnant women are dying because they are being denied the same health services as other women. . . .

Pregnant women in Peru die because they lack access to emergency obstetric care, to information on maternal health, and to health staff members who can speak indigenous languages such as Quechua—a native Andean language spoken by some 5 million people in Peru.

CNN.com,
"Peru Has High Maternal Mortality Rate, Rights Group Says,"
July 9, 2009. www.cnn.com.

Social and cultural discrimination against women increases their risk of sexual and reproductive health problems and hampers their ability to address them. For example, men in Peru frequently exercise control over their female partners' sexuality and fertility, expecting to be provided with sex on demand and opposing their use of contraception or barrier methods for infection prevention.[16,17] Male control is reinforced through intimate partner violence, which is commonplace. A recent prevalence study of gender-based violence found that half of all women in Lima, and almost two-thirds of all women in Cusco department reported having been physically and/or sexually abused by an intimate partner at least once in their lifetime.[18] . . .

Development of a Far Right Policy Approach: 2001–03

Between 2001 and 2003, progress in promoting reproductive health and rights in Peru was overshadowed when newly elected President Alejandro Toledo assumed office and appointed several ultra-conservatives to top government posts. For example, although the first Health Minister, Dr Luis Solari, only served in this position for six months, he filled key posts in the Ministry with opponents of reproductive choice, and left his colleague Dr Fernando Carbone at the helm of the MoH. Solari and Carbone both worked in concert with sympathetic legislators and with far right actors in the US such as Congressmen Chris Smith and Henry Hyde and US anti-choice groups, such as PRI and Human Life International.

The far right approach was not specific to Peru but part of a global fundamentalist movement of extremist groups from different religions, including Catholic, evangelical Christian and Muslim. According to a recent analysis of this period, the far right in Peru sought to apply strict interpretations of religious doctrine to broad-based public policies, with little regard for scientific or evidence-based interventions and no respect for individual choice. For example, all sexual relations—other than those between married heterosexual couples for the purpose of procreation—were characterised as immoral and sinful. Policy proposals stressed abstinence as the exclusive means to prevent STI/HIV transmission and natural methods for family planning. The far right position also held that an ideal family model, in which women's only role is motherhood, must be preserved at all costs.[8] Rather than promote gender equality and women's rights, policy proposals sought to reinforce women's subordination.

The three ministries responsible for social policy, MoH, MoEd and PROMUDEH (now MIMDES), removed all objectives and strategies designed to advance gender equity and sexual and reproductive health from existing and new policy documents. For example, the MoH's Health Policy Guidelines for 2002–12 contain no reference to gender inequity. Moreover, the Ministry of Education stopped providing sexual education and the MoH refused to make public any information on the family planning and gynaecological cancer programmes. The MoH eliminated its STI/AIDs control programme and put HIV prevention in a "Risk Reduction" programme that included malaria, dengue and other diseases.

Health Ministers Solari and Carbone worked to impede access to services and information on modern contraceptives, the use of condoms to protect against STIs and HIV, and to treat complications from unsafe abortion. Specific steps included directives discrediting critical reproductive technologies, spreading disinformation in the mass media, and blocking the distribution of needed supplies. For example, in early 2002, Carbone attempted to remove the IUD from the MoH protocol for contraceptive services on the basis that it was an abortifacient, while at the same time touting the effectiveness of the Billings method.[46] He also deterred the use of manual vacuum aspiration for post-abortion care, despite it being the safest available method for treating incomplete abortion and miscarriage.[46,47] In late 2002, health officials launched a disinformation campaign on condoms, characterising them as totally ineffective in preventing STIs and HIV because they contain spermicides. Around this same time, the monitoring efforts carried out by the Public Ombudsman's office uncovered evidence of barriers imposed by health services to prevent women from obtaining contraceptive methods.[48] Evidence from two recent studies confirm the negative impact of these policies, including decreases in access to and use of modern contraceptives and increased reliance on "natural" methods and unsafe abortion.[10,49]

International donors have effectively been prevented from supporting reproductive health and rights in Peru since 2001. This has been compounded by the fact that both USAID and UNFPA have been under siege by reproductive rights opponents in the US Congress. The Bush administration itself has been working actively to undermine reproductive health programmes such as Peru's globally,[50] and US foreign policy for

Peru has changed from prioritising democracy and human rights to the war on drugs. Pursuing this goal has required Peru's full cooperation with the US State Department to design and implement an aggressive counternarcotics strategy with little local input.[51] USAID has also reshaped its entire development portfolio in seven coca-growing states.[52] Confidential sources report that US officials in Peru have expressed willingness to sacrifice reproductive health assistance to appease the right and maintain good relations with the Toledo government.

In fact, USAID/Peru has limited its support for interventions to address unwanted pregnancy and unsafe abortion. Emergency contraception is a clear example. In 1992, emergency contraception was approved in Peru, though not distributed.* However, after USAID/Peru was first attacked by the far right in early 1998, officials responded by pressuring the MoH to remove emergency contraception from the approved list. In 2001, when the transitional government was in office, civil society organisations convinced health officials to reincorporate emergency contraception, for which USAID provided technical assistance.[53]

However, USAID's support for emergency contraception was short-lived.[54] Under Toledo, health ministers Solari and Carbone refused to make it available in public health clinics, claiming it was abortifacient. This not only blocked USAID/Peru's support for public provision but also had a chilling effect on their support to the NGO and private sectors to integrate emergency contraception into their programmes. USAID/Peru has also refused to lend seed money needed to market Postinor-2, an emergency contraceptive product distributed by the social marketing organisation, *Apprende*, since 2002. US anti-choice pressure also remains high. In 2002, on a

---

* The following methods are also approved: IUD, male condom, oral contraceptives, injectables, Norplant, male and female sterilisation, vaginal suppositories, and rhythm/ calendar and Billings methods. The diaphragm and the female condom have still not been incorporated into the method mix.

visit to Peru, US Congressman Chris Smith threatened USAID officials, "You better not be funding emergency contraception here."[54] Finally, political appointees at USAID in Washington have withdrawn institutional backing for emergency contraception, even if technical staff continue to favour the method. So although it remains an approved method in Peru and in the US, USAID/Peru will not support it.

Current Context

During his first two years in office, President Toledo avoided publicly declaring his government's position on reproductive health and rights. In July 2003, after consistent pressure from women's groups, reproductive health and HIV/AIDS organisations and progressive medical associations, Toledo publicly resolved to back family planning policies according to the World Health Organization guidelines. He also replaced ultra-conservative cabinet members, including Health Minister Carbone, with professionals who endorse evidenced-based policies regarding reproductive health and rights.

Not surprisingly, far right leaders, particularly in the congress, continue to put intense pressure on the MoH to limit access to reproductive health services and technologies. Ultra-conservatives joined forces to have Chávez Chuchón appointed to the chair of the Congressional Health Committee for 2003–04. However, the current health minister, Dr Pilar Mazzetti, a neurologist appointed to the post in February 2004, is standing firm to reverse the far right policies in the MoH, taking concrete steps to improve sexual and reproductive health services, information and education and engage with civil society. For example, in July 2004, the MoH launched a new "Programme of Integrated Care in Sexual and Reproductive Health" and approved new national guidelines for services.[55] In addition, Dr Mazzetti responded resolutely to the disinformation campaign launched by the far right against emergency contraception, based on the scientific evidence that the method is not an abortifacient, and announced that it will at last be distributed in MoH services.[55] Finally, Dr Mazzetti met with 15 organisations from the *Mesa de Vigilancia en Derechos Sexuales y Reproductivos*, to discuss ways in which this civil society coalition can help promote sustainable public policies in sexual and reproductive health.

Conclusion

In spite of their contradictory nature, the demographic and far right policy approaches share an important characteristic: they are clearly not compatible with gender equality or reproductive rights and hinder progress toward achieving these goals in concrete ways. Under the demographic approach, many health care providers throughout Peru were pressured to perform sterilisations under inadequate conditions and without complying with standards of informed consent, or lose their posts. Meanwhile, under the far right approach, health care providers were discouraged from delivering modern contraceptives, condoms and post-abortion care. These policy approaches are the greatest obstacles to making real and long-lasting improvements to sexual and reproductive health and rights.

Acknowledgements

I am grateful to the following people for reviewing this article: María Cristina Arismendy, formerly with UNFPA/Peru; Susana Chávez, Centro de la Mujer Peruana Flora Tristán; Milka Dinev, Pathfinder International Peru; Dr Ana Güezmes, Observatorio del Derecho a la Salud, Consorcio de Investigación Ecónomica y Social; and Dr Luis Távara, Sociedad Peruana de Obstetricia y Ginecología. I also want to thank colleagues who read the full report: Frescia Carrasco, Movimiento Manuela Ramos; Federico León, formerly Population Council Peru; Richard Martin, USAID/Peru; Shira Saperstein, Moriah Fund; and Alicia Yamin, international consultant. The views expressed in this article are those of the author alone. I also appreciate helpful insights and guidance from Jodi L Jacobson and Rupsa Mallik, CHANGE.

References

1. Aramburu C. Is population policy necessary? Latin America and the Andean countries. In: Population and Development Review 1994;20(Suppl.): 159–78.

2. Reyes J, Ochoa LH. Informe Principal de la Encuesta Demográfica y de Salud Familiar 1996. Lima: Instituto Nacional de Estadística e Informática, 1997.

3. Mannarelli ME. Diagnóstico de Salud Reproductiva en el Perú. Proyecto: Seguimiento del Programa de Acción de la Conferencia Internacional de Población y Desarrollo, El Cairo, 1994. Lima: Movimiento Manuela Ramos, Centro de la Mujer Peruana Flora Tristán, 1997.

4. Murrillo Hernández R. Informe: Balance del grado de cumplimiento de la Plataforma de Acción Mundial en el Perú. A cinco años de la IV Conferencia Internacional sobre la Mujer. Lima: Grupo Impulsor Nacional Mujeres para la Igualdad Real, 2000.

5. Dador J, Chávez S, Gutiérrez R, et al. Derechos de las Mujeres y Equidad de Género: Estado Actual de su Cumplimiento por el Estado Peruano. Lima: Movimiento Manuela Ramos, 2001.

6. Tamayo G. Nada Personal: Reporte de Derechos Humanos sobre la Aplicación de la Anticoncepción Quirúrgica en el Perú 1996–1998. Lima: Comité de América Latina y el Caribe para la Defensa de los Derechos de la Mujer, 1999.

7. Villanueva R. Anticoncepción quirúrgica voluntaria I: casos investigados por la Defensoría del Pueblo. Serie Informes Defensoriales No 7. Lima: Defensoría del Pueblo, 1998.

8. Chávez S with Cisneros R. Cuando los fundamentalismos se apoderan de las políticas públicas. Lima: Centro de la Mujer Peruana Flora Tristán, 2004.

9. Távara L, Sasca D, Frisancho O, et al., Estado actual de la mortalidad materna en los hospitales del Perú. Ginecología y Obstetricia (Perú) 1999;45: 38–42.

10. Ferrando D. El aborto clandestino en el Perú. Nuevas Evidencias. Lima: Centro de la Mujer Peruana Flora Tristán, Pathfinder International, 2004.

11. Ferrando D. El aborto clandestino en el Perú. Hechos y cifras. Lima: Centro de la Mujer Peruana Flora Tristán, Pathfinder International, 2002.

12. Reyes J, Ochoa LH. Informe principal de la Encuesta Demográfica y de Salud Familiar 2000. Lima: Instituto Nacional de Estadística e Informática, 2001.

13. Sánchez J, Gotuzzo E, Escamilla J, et al. Gender differences in sexual practices and sexually transmitted infections among adults in Lima, Peru. American Journal of Public Health 1996;86:1098–1107.

14. Noriega M. Lejos de las garras de Sida. Diario El Comercio, 4 March 2001. Section F, p.4.

15. Dirección de Programas Sociales. Plan Nacional de Prevención del Cáncer Ginecológico: Cuello Uterino y Mama 1998–2000. Lima: Ministerio de Salud, 1999.

16. Garate MR, Salazar X, Cobían E, et al. Hombres Como Socios en Salud, Lima: Population Council, 1998.

17. Fuller N. Cambios y continuidades en la identidad masculina: varones en Lima, Cuzco e Iquitos. Paper presented at VI Congreso Latino-Americano de Ciencias Sociales y Salud, Lima, 10–13 June 2001.

18. Güezmes A, Palomino N, Ramos M. Violencia Sexual y Física contra las Mujeres en el Perú. Estudio multicéntrico de la OMS sobre la violencia de pareja y la salud de las

mujeres. Lima: Centro de la Mujer Peruana Flora Tristán, Universidad Peruana Cayetano Heredia, World Health Organization, 2002. . . .

46. Carbone F. Memorandum No. 012-2002-MINSA sent to the Dirección General de Salud de las Personas. Lima: Ministerio de Salud, 1 April 2002.

47. Carbone F. Communiqué published in various daily newspapers. Lima: Ministerio de Salud, 28 May 2002.

48. Villanueva R, Ramos M, Velazsco K, et a1. La aplicación de la anticoncepción quirúrgica voluntaria y los derechos reproductivos III: casos investigados por la Defensoría del Pueblo, Serie Informes Defensoriales No. 69. Lima: Defensoría del Pueblo, 2002.

49. Suberia G. Disponibilidad asegurada de insumos anticonceptivos: derecho y responsabilidad de todos. Resumen ejecutivo. Lima: Policy Project, 2004.

50. Marshall E. La otra guerra de Bush. Ataque contra la salud y los derechos sexuales y reproductivos de las mujeres. New York: International Women's Health Coalition, 2004.

51. Coe A with Jacobson J. Memorandum to USAID/Peru on the implications of its coca-eradication strategy for USAID's health, family planning and nutrition programs, Takoma Park MD: Center for Health and Gender Equity, 30 October 2003.

52. Integrated Development Programme. Weekly and bi-weekly progress reports. Lima: USAID/Peru, 2003–2004.

53. Martin R. Letter to the Center for Health and Gender Equity. Lima: USAID/Peru, 15 June 2001.

54. Coe A. Informing Choices: Expanding Access to Emergency Contraception in Peru, Takoma Park MD: Center for Health and Gender Equity, 2002.

55. Aseguran que debate por la AOE ya terminó. Diario Perú 21. 18 July 2004. p.14.

Iran's Islamic Republic Is Credited for Success in Reducing Overpopulation

Alvaro Serrano

Iran's population exploded in the late 1970s and early mid-1980s, leading to a change in thinking among government leaders, reports Alvaro Serrano in the following viewpoint. The high growth rates challenged the country to meet its citizens' needs, he asserts, and a meeting in 1988 brought agreement that smaller families would be good for the nation. According to Serrano, members of the Islamic clergy gave their full support to all methods of family planning. The campaign to reduce population growth was successful due to high literacy rates that made a media campaign and education effective, he argues. Iran also had the health care infrastructure necessary to give people access to contraceptive methods. Slower population growth helped the country invest more in its health care system. The United Nations Population Fund (UNFPA) helps countries use population data to make decisions that impact poverty and support safe and wanted births. Serrano is a communications advisor at the United Nations Population Fund.

As you read, consider the following questions:

1. On average, how many births per woman does Alvaro Serrano say there were in Iran in 2005?

Alvaro Serrano, "A Holistic Approach Underpins the Islamic Republic of Iran's Success in Family Planning," United Nations Population Fund, February 9, 2006. Reproduced by permission.

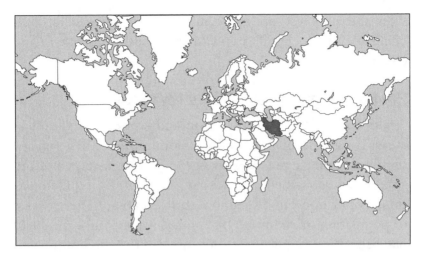

2. According to the author, how much did the Iranian population grow between 1979 and 1986?

3. What family size were Iranian couples encouraged to observe by the media campaign?

The Islamic Republic of Iran is a textbook example of how rapidly fertility rates can change in a supportive environment. Elements of Iran's success in reducing fertility include a strong national consensus (forged with the help of Islamic clergy) to meet the economic needs of the population, strategic and concerted policies that link resources to population dynamics, and accessible reproductive health services offering a wide mix of contraceptive options.

The Islamic Republic of Iran's success in family planning—which led to the dramatic decline in fertility from more than six children on average in the early 1980s to just over two births per woman in 2005—has been called that country's 'other revolution.' Many of the strategies mapped out decades ago to address the country's swelling population—including a strong network of rural health centres, mandatory premarital counselling on family planning and free family planning services and supplies—are still contributing to the general well-being of Iranian families and to the health of mothers and children.

Political Commitment Drives Changes

"Iran's success story in population and reproductive health is a vivid example of how political commitment, in its broad sense, can bring about a sea change in development in a record time," said Mohamed Abdel-Ahad, the UNFPA [United Nations Population Fund] country representative. "The embrace of population programmes by political leaders since the 1980s has been the driving force for community mobilization, resource allocation and overcoming sociocultural barriers to reproductive health and family planning," he added.

In the early 1980s, just after the Islamic revolution with the war with Iraq still unfolding, large families were considered an advantage and were encouraged by the Iranian government. Between 1979 and 1986, the population shot up from 34 to 49 million, due to the combination of high birthrates, reduced mortality and an influx of refugees. A huge 'baby boom', with long-lasting impact on the country's demographic structure, occurred during that period. Then came a 180-degree turnaround, in both government thinking and in fertility rates.

High Population Growth Hindered the Ability of the Government

By 1988, the government planners had become convinced that high growth rates were undermining the country's ability to meet the needs of its people, especially given the costs of reconstruction following the war. A three-day seminar on population and development in 1988 helped convince the country's leadership, the clergy and the media that smaller families are good for individuals and society as a whole. A crucial element in the country's success was gaining the full support of Islamic clergy. Edicts from religious leaders declared that all methods of family planning, including sterilization, conformed to Islamic principles.

A broad media campaign encouraged couples to delay their first pregnancy, space births and limit family size to three children. High literacy rates made it easier to spread the message. Premarital counselling, which includes information about contraception for both men and women, was made a requirement for registering for marriage. Population education was integrated into all levels of the education system. Many of the economic incentives for large families were removed.

"We have the religious leaders aware and involved, there is political will, there is programming and there is infrastructure."

At the same time, the country was able to take advantage of its well-developed health infrastructure to provide married couples with easy access to modern contraceptive methods. They were available free of charge at public clinics. An innovative rural health care network, staffed by local health providers, known as *behvarzes*, helped meet the needs of the widely dispersed rural population, and mobile clinics reached populations in very remote areas. Women Health Volunteers managed to get family planning information to other hard-to-reach segments of the population.

The country's progress in reducing fertility is very much in line with the multipronged approach promoted by Dr. M. E. Akbari, former Undersecretary for Health and his predecessors in that position. Successful initiatives, Dr. Akbari noted, need to be broad-based and holistic, backed up by supportive policies and programming. That was the case for the country's success with family planning, he said. "We have the religious

---

Abortion Laws in Iran

Abortion has been illegal in Iran since the 1979 Islamic Revolution. Although there are no explicit exceptions to this prohibition, Iranian law generally allows acts that are performed to save the life of a person; thus, it is commonly understood that abortion is illegal except when necessary to save the mother's life. In 2005, the Iranian parliament passed a measure allowing abortions within the first four months of pregnancy in cases of fetal impairment that would result in economic burden; the measure was ultimately blocked by the Iranian Guardian Council.

The Pew Forum,
Abortion Laws Around the World,
September 30, 2008. http://pewforum.org.

---

leaders aware and involved, there is political will, there is programming and there is infrastructure."

Slower Population Growth Supports Progress

The slower growth in the Iranian population over the last 15 years has made progress on a number of other fronts possible. The country has been able to invest more in its primary health care system. Maintaining the new cultural norm for small families is important to avoid a second population surge as the Iranian baby boomers (those born between 1979 and 1989) enter their prime reproductive years.

UNFPA has long been a strategic partner of the Islamic Republic of Iran, providing financial and technical support to its ambitious family planning programme. With the country's fertility rate now close to, or even at, replacement level, UNFPA's support has shifted toward other issues, including addressing the reproductive health needs of men and unmarried adolescents, who are not covered by the current primary health care system, and improving information and services to prevent HIV and other sexually transmitted infections. However, the government is aware of the need to maintain its success in family planning, especially because of the large numbers of young people in or approaching their reproductive years.

The country is also interested in sharing the lessons it has learned with neighbouring countries, said Mr. Abdel-Ahad. "UNFPA is working closely with the government and civil society to document Iran's experience and share it with the rest of the world utilizing south-south cooperation modalities," he noted.

China's Cultural Traditions Impact Working Women's Reproductive Equality

Asia Monitor Resource Centre

According to the Asia Monitor Resource Centre, Chinese society underwent a rapid transformation in the early 1980s and the social safety net, designed around little population movement and social change, could not keep pace. A public welfare void has developed that impacts the reproductive rights and health of working women, claims the Asia Monitor Resource Centre in this viewpoint. Data gathered in a survey of garment industry workers revealed that policies for working women were unequally applied. Women often are not allowed protection while pregnant, and many managers are not receptive to accommodating women's health needs, asserts the author. Many women also had little understanding about the health risks of AIDS. Asia Monitor Resource Centre focuses on Asian labor concerns; provides research, education, and training; and supports campaigns by its regional partners.

As you read, consider the following questions:

1. How many useable questionnaires did the Pearl River Delta survey generate?
2. What percentage of women reported that wages were higher for men working in their factory?

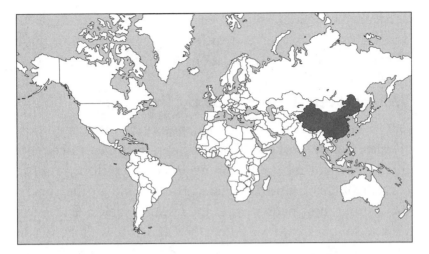

3. According to the survey results, how many women said their factories imposed limits on using the bathroom?

After new China was founded, a social welfare system was put in place based on the administrative separation of city and country. Under this system, the reproductive health and rights of women workers in the cities were protected through their work unit. In the countryside, women's reproductive health and rights were given some kind of guarantee under a system of cooperatives. This system presupposed extremely little population movement and social change. But after 1978 the economy liberalized and state-owned enterprises were reformed. Rural people began leaving their homes to seek employment elsewhere, and a new term entered in the Chinese vocabulary: *dagong* [meaning "to work" and usually associated with migrant workers]. Chinese society underwent a sudden transformation, and social welfare had no way to keep up with the pace of change. Within this public welfare "void," the reproductive health and rights of working women are being seriously violated. Moreover, these rights are seriously limited by China's policies of population control.

A sample survey was carried out in the garment industry in China's Pearl River Delta. This survey sought to better understand the situation of women workers' reproductive health and rights, analyze several different factors affecting these rights, and make recommendations for further action.

Women Were Interviewed by Their Peers

Data were gathered using participatory research methods. Women factory workers themselves were recruited to conduct interviews, and received training in survey techniques. The content of this training included background to the survey, the relevant information about the research subject, and interview techniques etcetera. Altogether 22 workers took part in the interviewer training. They conducted surveys simultaneously in five cities: Guangzhou, Shenzhen (inner and outer zones), Dongguan, Fuoshan and Huizhou. They relied on personal introductions to meet interviewees, and also approached other workers at random outside their factory compounds. They had no access to detailed factories documents. The sample yielded from this method is potentially insufficient. To improve the accuracy of results, an equal number of interviews were conducted in each city, factory, and work department.

The survey yielded 277 useable questionnaires, from 62 factories in five cities. On average, four to five interviews were conducted per factory. . . . 29.2% of interviewees were from Shenzhen, which is balanced if one considers Shenzhen's inner and outer zones as two quite different working environments. . . .

The survey showed that most women workers had attained a junior high school education. As for interviewees' ages and educational backgrounds:

- 71.5% of respondents were between 21 and 35 years old.

- 15.2% were between 16 and 20 years old.

- 28.9% only completed primary school.

- 61.4% had completed up until the end of junior high school.

The recent labor shortage in the Pearl River Delta has meant that migrant women are spending longer periods of time *dagong* than in previous times. Because they are spending more years working in the cities, their marriages and childbearing are being increasingly influenced by life in factories. 39.7% of interviewees had never married, 59.2% were married, and 0.7% had been divorced.

91% of interviewees came from provinces outside Guangdong. Because of the nature of China's current system, migrant workers' living expenses are higher than local residents. These high costs mean that workers eventually have to return to their home towns. In our survey, only 13.2% of interviewees were over 36 years of age. Older migrant women have gone home.

"Because [migrant women] are spending more years working in the cities, their marriages and childbearing are being increasingly influenced by life in factories."

Policies Vary Widely from Pregnant Women

In 1988 the Chinese national government enacted the *Regulation on Protecting Women Workers*. In 1994, the National Labour Bureau released the *Trial Regulations on Protecting Women's Reproductive Health*, followed by regulations to protect women workers enacted by provincial and local governments. But basically these regulations have not been implemented or adhered to.

In this survey, no respondent was able to say with certainty that their employer had bought maternity insurance for them. Women do not receive the kind of protection they should, but rather receive all kinds of unfair treatment. Only 2.5% of survey respondents said with certainty that pregnant women at their workplaces were allowed to take health checks in work time. 40.4% said that this was not allowed, and 53.8% did not know. 7.2% said that their factory provided time and facilities for breast-feeding. 9.7% said that pregnant women were still allocated overtime, and in these factories, 70.4% of pregnant women worked the same amount of overtime as their nonpregnant coworkers. Two interviewees said that pregnant women at their factories were still allocated the night shift.

Because of this, many women leave and come back to work in factories after returning to their home towns to give birth. At surveyed factories, 66.1% had women who chose to resign their jobs after falling pregnant. 21.1% were unable to receive the wages owed to them at the time they resigned. Furthermore, 1.4% received no compensation when made redundant after becoming pregnant.

"9.7% [of interviewees] said that pregnant women were still allocated overtime, and in these factories, 70.4% of pregnant women worked the same amount of overtime as their nonpregnant coworkers."

Nonetheless, there are some factories that provide women workers with some degree of protection. 33.9% of interviewees said that pregnant women in their factories could continue working up until the time of delivery, and then take 90 days paid maternity leave. 1.4% (four people) said that pregnant women can take leave if they miscarry or have an abortion.

Of all 277 respondents, 10.5% (29 women) had been pregnant before while working at a garment factory. None of them had maternity insurance, or had it provided by their employer. But some of these women did receive some protection.

Some were able to continue working right up until the time of delivery, and then take maternity leave. Only some could take paid maternity leave. Some factories, however, were really awful. Those bosses do not give pregnant women any extra rest time, relief from strenuous work, or health checks. Because of the health complications of work under these circumstances, many of these women choose to quit work until after giving birth. Of the 29 interviewees who had been pregnant at a garment factory, nine quit their jobs after falling pregnant, four of whom could not claim wages owed to them. Four had to keep working overtime while pregnant. 14 were exposed to hazardous substances or practices. . . . Four women miscarried because work time was too long, pressure too great, or because of accidents. Two women's babies were stillborn.

Not All Women Were in Control of Their Sexual Health

99 interviewees (37.5%) had no experience with sex. By contrast, 110 women were married (39.7%). Interviewees had quite conservative attitudes to sex.

Of the 170 respondents with sexual experience (excluding eight women who did not answer questions in this section) 90% took measures to prevent pregnancy. Intrauterine coils were most widely used, used by 66.5%. Only 10.6% used condoms, and 5.9% the contraceptive pill. Only 20 women (11.8%) choose for their partner to be the one to acquire contraceptive devices, or for the two of them to take responsibility together. That means that remaining 90% or so take responsibility for conception on their own, and bear the consequences of its failure.

Contraception does not always work. Of the 153 women who practiced contraception, 15 (9.8%) had experienced accidental pregnancy: five because of problems with condoms, four because they forgot to take the pill on time, three because they miscalculated the "safe period" in their menstrual cycle, two because their intrauterine coils became dislodged, and two did not know the reason. Of the 17 sexually active respondents who did not practice contraception, three (7.6%) have been pregnant before. All these 15 women who had accidentally become pregnant chose to abort. None of them took leave from work.

Almost 40% of interviewees have experienced irregular periods. Some have had irregular cycles, some experience unusual pain, and some had experienced noticeable increases or decreases in bleeding. 22 (20.2%) said that they go to work with serious period pain. 29 (26.6%) said that they don't dare ask their manager for time off because of period pain. Furthermore, 30.3% are anemic.

Our survey included questions about AIDS. We found that only 1.4% of respondents were at . . . [relatively] familiar with the disease. 9.7% did not know what AIDS was, and 38.3% thought that it had nothing to [do] with them.

Little Protection from Hazards Exists in the Workplace

In this survey, the main hazard that women faced at work was dust (for example, cloth fibres and hairs), noise, and high work pressure. 74.4% said that they came into contact with dust, 62.5% with noise, and 56.5% with high work pressure. 34.7% reported eye strain, and 33.9% muscle strain because of repetitive movement. 27.8% of workers felt that their workshop was either too hot or too cold. For these questions, interviewees could select more than one work hazard.

Of those women exposed to these workplace hazards, not many were provided with personal protective equipment (PPE). 33.3% had protection for chemical substances, but some thought that it was inadequate. 36.4% had equipment to protect them from muscle strain, but only 25% thought that it was sufficient. 30.5% were provided with equipment to protect their eyes, but 6.9% felt it was inadequate.

China's One-Child Policy Has Degraded Women's Reproductive Rights

The one-child policy was devised in the 1970s to curb China's burgeoning population, now [August 2008] at more than 1.3 billion, but the implementation has resulted in numerous human rights violations. Women who have refused to have abortions, sterilizations, and/or use contraception, as well as their family members, have been threatened, lost jobs and homes, and have been imprisoned. Local authorities who decide when and how to collect the so-called "social maintenance" penalties used to enforce the one-child policy, and these fines have often been abusive, arbitrary, and corrupt. . . .

China's growing gender-ratio disparity is a result of the restrictive implementation of its family planning policies and the deep cultural prevalence for male children. Some officials have admitted that the one-child policy has "aggravated the imbalance," as the restrictions have led to sex selective abortions that have overwhelmingly caused the abortion of female fetuses.

Marcy Bloom,
"Behind the Spectacle: Women's Human Rights in China,"
RH Reality Check, August 19, 2008. www.rhrealitycheck.org.

There is still not enough priority placed on occupational safety and health (OSH). Only 19.4% of workers had any protection from dust, 11% from noise damage, and 9.3% from the high pressure of their work. 35% of interviewees felt that their protection from dust was inadequate. 15.8% thought they did not have enough protection from noise, and 46.2% from work pressure.

Factories Demand Documents from Women

45.8% of women interviewed reported that the wages were higher for male workers at their factory than women, and that men and women generally hold different kinds of positions.

When workers enter a new factory they often have to provide documents to factory management. Besides the national ID card, which is required by law, all other documents the factory demands for its own purposes. When entering their current factory, 99.2% of interviewees in this survey had to provide their national ID card, 35.3% had to provide their migrant family planning and marriage certificate, 20.2% had to provide a certificate certifying that they were not married, and 13% had to provide a marriage certificate. Certain women may receive some particular treatment from management because of their marriage or family status.

Moreover, in the general comments section of the survey, 1.1% of respondents indicated that they had to produce a "labor service certificate" (*laowuzheng*), 0.4% had to produce an employment certificate, 0.4% had to provide a photograph, and 0.7% had to provide a certificate of good health.

"Certain women may receive some particular treatment from management because of their marriage or family status."

Perhaps for some people, the freedom to use the bathroom is perfectly reasonable. But for 22.4% of women surveyed (62 people), their factories imposed limits on use of the bathroom. Two women do not even receive leniency when they are menstruating or pregnant. That is to say that in the garment industry, one in five women cannot freely use the bathroom.

Negligence Has Spawned Gaps in Rights and Knowledge

Our survey results indicate that there are still gaps in the protection of women's reproductive health and rights. Their special needs at work are ignored, particularly during their menstrual period. Work and childbirth are both normal parts of life, but as far as many women garment workers are concerned, these two things are major contradictions in their lives.

These survey results have painted a frightening picture. The current situation is the product of harsh management models and negligent attitudes on the part of government and society. At the same time, women workers have inadequate knowledge about reproductive health and little concept of their rights, which makes them vulnerable to abuse.

On the other hand, the survey did reveal that in some places women have been granted protection of their reproductive health and rights, including maternity insurance and leave.

"The current situation is the product of harsh management models and negligent attitudes on the part of government and society."

Recommendations:

1. The government must fulfil its responsibility, and urge employers to buy maternity insurance for their female employees.

2. Women should receive more information and training about their reproductive health and rights.

Periodical Bibliography

The following articles have been selected to supplement the diverse views presented in this chapter.

Marleen Bosmans, Dina Nasser, Umaiyeh Khammash, Patricia Claeys, and Marleen Temmerman — "Palestinian Women's Sexual and Reproductive Health Rights in a Longstanding Humanitarian Crisis," *Reproductive Health Matters*, May 2008.

Cynthia Ingar — "Midwifery and Birthing: Women in Peru," *Midwifery Today*, Spring 2008.

Edgar Kestler, Beatriz Barrios, Elsa M. Hernández, Vinicio del Valle, and Alejandro Silva — "Humanizing Access to Modern Contraceptive Methods in National Hospitals in Guatemala, Central America," *Contraception*, July 2009.

Sepali Kottegoda, Kumudini Samuel, Sarala Emmanuel — "Reproductive Health Concerns in Six Conflict-Affected Areas of Sri Lanka," *Reproductive Health Matters*, May 2008.

Siobhán Mullaly — "Debating Reproductive Rights in Ireland," *Human Rights Quarterly*, February 2005.

Emily Rauhala — "The Philippines' Birth Control Battle," *Time*, June 6, 2008.

Sandra Reineke — "*In Vitro Veritas*: New Reproductive and Genetic Technologies and Women's Rights in Contemporary France," *International Journal of Feminist Approaches to Bioethics*, Spring 2008.

Amy Stillman — "Chávez Is Failing Women," *New Statesman*, August 27, 2009.

Humayun Kabir Tutul — "Human Trafficking in Bangladesh and Beyond," Common Ground News Service, September 30, 2008. www.commongroundnews.org.

GLOBALVIEWPOINTS

CHAPTER

Women's Social Rights

Germany Responds to an Afghan Girl's Murder in the Name of Honor

Barbara Hans

According to Barbara Hans in the following viewpoint, the violent stabbing of a sixteen-year-old Afghan girl by her brother brought outrage and calls for German society to ramp up its efforts to stop so-called "honor killings." The girl's adoption of Western styles and standards had created tension in her family, and the young woman had sought refuge from them, says Hans. Women's rights activists say the term "honor killing" must be rejected. Also, Hans asserts, young women who break from their families must be provided adequate protection. Spiegel Online is the Web presence of Der Spiegel, *the most widely read news magazine in Germany. Hans is a journalist for* Der Spiegel.

As you read, consider the following questions:

1. According to the United Nations, how many women fall victim to honor killings worldwide each year?

2. How old was the man who stabbed his sister?

3. What is the name of the organization in Berlin that helps girls who are being hunted by their families?

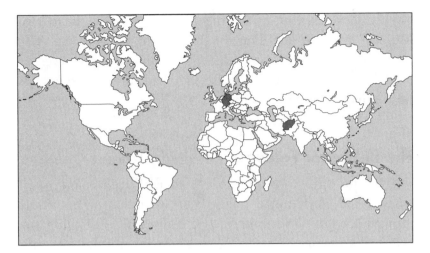

Ahmad O. stabbed his sister more than 20 times because the 16-year-old girl didn't live her life according to his values. Women's rights advocate Seyran Ates is now calling for German society to intensify its efforts to stop honor killings. "A girl isn't a whore if she goes out," she says.

Morsal O. was 16, a young girl with joie de vivre [joy of living]. She laughed a lot and she was a go-getter. She was a good student, had ambition and a lot ahead of her in life. But she was murdered on Friday, May 9 [2008]. Her 23-year-old brother Ahmad, with the help of a cousin, lured her to a parking lot near a subway station in the German port city of Hamburg under a false pretense and stabbed her 20 times with a knife.

If Morsal had known she would be coming face to face with her brother, she probably wouldn't have gone that evening. The two hadn't been on talking terms for quite some time, and Ahmad had threatened his sister repeatedly. Just before her murder, Morsal had sought refuge from her family, who moved to Germany from Afghanistan 13 years ago, at a number of city social facilities, most recently living for more than a year in a youth safe house. But she never succeeded in entirely breaking off contact with her family.

For more than an hour, emergency doctors fought to save Morsal's life, but she died on the way to the hospital. The girl's parents rushed to the scene, but they weren't allowed to attend to their daughter because they had forgotten their IDs in the midst of the turmoil.

Morsal died alone.

The Desire for Freedom Results in Tragedy

"Maybe he did it out of love," Morsal's cousin Mudja said, when asked why Ahmad stabbed his sister that night. Mudja O. gave an extensive interview to *Spiegel TV* following the crime, discussing the stabbing and her cousin's possible motives for the killing. "We spoke to him and he told us, 'My sisters are my life. She should be put away before anything happens to her.' The last sentence that we heard from him was that he loved his sister."

It was not the first time Ahmad, who worked in an auto parts store, had come to the attention of the police for violent acts, either. In police circles, he was known as a serial offender, constantly in trouble for beatings and even stabbings. Morsal had even tried to get charges pressed against her brother with the police after he repeatedly attacked her, but she later withdrew them.

"There were constant fights because she wore too much makeup, or didn't come home when she was told to, . . . didn't do enough homework or had the wrong friends."

In the *Spiegel TV* interview, her cousin says that Morsal "simply wanted more freedom." She wanted to lead her own life and not the one her parents had planned for her. "She was actually given a lot of freedom, in my opinion. She had some piercings, for example. Her parents didn't say anything about it. She could wear what she wanted—even if she wasn't allowed to wear a miniskirt to school."

Morsal had tried to test her limits—they were sometimes very narrow at home. For Morsal they were too narrow even if the 16-year-old dressed like a Western girl, with tight jeans and colorful shirts.

There were constant fights because she wore too much makeup, or didn't come home when she was told to, because she locked herself in her room, didn't do enough homework or had the wrong friends. Ahmad thought it was his duty to take care of his sister. He observed what she was doing closely. He was worried, his cousin says. If he couldn't keep an eye on her, he had some other member of the extended family do it for him. Cousins, second cousins, uncles and aunts, the network of relations was tight-knit—and big.

Honor Killings Must Be Rejected by the Public

Morsal tried to protect herself from these restrictions, her cousin recalls. She managed to almost completely avoid Ahmad and she no longer spoke with him. "He tried again and again and he failed. At some stage the parents stepped in and said, 'That's enough, this is our daughter.'"

The trouble never let up, though, and Morsal eventually moved into a youth safe house. Her lifestyle, her concept of freedom and self-expression didn't chime with her family's. Tradition was very important to Ahmad, and he didn't want Morsal to be out and about at all hours of the day. "He was worried when he didn't know where his sister was. He didn't want to get a call at 1 A.M. and be told his sister was lying beaten up on the street. He was expecting something like that," his cousin says, attempting to explain something she herself cannot really understand.

According to a United Nations report, around 5,000 women fall victim to "honor killings" around the world each year. The true figure, however, is most likely much higher. Between January 1996 and July 2005, 55 honor killings were reported to the police in Germany alone. Yet it is difficult to record the crime because there is no official police definition.

"We have to stop talking about 'so-called honor killings,'" lawyer and women's rights activist Seyran Ates told *Spiegel Online*. "There is no such thing. These are not 'so-called' honor killings, but plain and simple honor killings. This term 'honor' is based on a woman not being allowed to express her own sexuality. It means: no premarital sex, no boyfriend. If a girl or young woman doesn't stick to this then she is seen as a scourge—someone who must be killed in order to restore honor."

Honor can be washed clean with the blood of the "guilty one," she explains. "The term 'honor,' that honor killings are based upon, has nothing at all to do with the Western understanding of the word," says Ates. "And it can only be overcome by publicly rejecting it. Children have to be taught in school that this term is dehumanizing. We have to take a stand within society. We have to make it very clear: 'If you think like this, then you are living in the wrong century. You are breaking the rules of the constitutional state in which you live, and you are not respecting human or women's rights.'"

Ahmad's parents have already distanced themselves from their son. In an interview with German public broadcaster NDR, his father said: "My son is a criminal," and his mother said, "I hate him." The police are investigating how much Ahmad's family might have known about his murderous plan, but they haven't found any incriminating evidence so far.

Education and Protection Are Needed

But Ates says that those who carry out honor killings should also be considered victims. "The men are one part of a system," she says. "A 23-year-old man is driven to brutally stab his sister to death. But he was not born a murderer. We have to reflect on what pushed him so far."

In Jordan, It Is Difficult to Account for Honor Crimes

Official statistics indicate that the majority of women killed in honor crimes are predominantly teenagers. Most are buried in unmarked graves, disgraced even in death.

Jordan has one of the lowest rates of homicide; however, a 1998 United Nations [UN] study of official figures from the mid 1990s showed that murder was the most frequent crime against women, and the honor crimes (including murder and accidental murder) accounted for [the] largest category—55%—[of reported] violence, especially if perpetrated by a member of the family.

The UN estimates 5,000 a year (victims, but not necessarily killed) categorized as follows:

- Permitted under Jordanian law, articles 98 and 340;

- Usually carried out by father or brother of victim;

- Partner faces penalties if victim found not to have been virgin.

Additionally, there is an average of 25 crimes in Jordan occurring every year, clearly as honor crimes. Almost 99% of these crimes target women only. However, [there are a] number of honor crime cases that are categorized under other reasons such as suicides or accidents.

Lubna Dawany Nimry,
"Crimes of Honor in Jordan and the Arab World,"
Civil Society Development Center, June 2009, pp. 11–12.
www.stgm.org.tr.

This perverted understanding of honor needs to be dealt with critically while these men are still in school, and awareness of the issue has to be raised within the legal profession, where many of these cases are handled, she argues. In particular, work needs to be done to raise awareness among families. "It needs to be communicated to families that their daughter is not a whore if she goes out in the evening. We have to tell families: 'Whatever your daughter does, whether she takes drugs, or has a boyfriend, or gets involved in crime—no one has the right to kill her.'"

If a girl turns away from her family, then it is vitally important that she is given protection and that someone accompanies her if she contacts her family. In Berlin the Papatya Project helps girls who are being hunted by their families. Papatya has no official address and cannot be directly contacted by telephone—in order to protect the young women. Contact is established through aid organizations and youth welfare services. People who work with the girls say that they are rarely aware of the danger their relatives can pose and often meet with their fathers, brothers, or cousins. "We advise the girls not to leave the house during the first few days. We have a lot of girls who are in danger, and who don't go outside for weeks at a time," one of the project staff told *Spiegel Online*.

"This perverted understanding of honor needs to be dealt with critically while these men are still in school, and awareness of the issue has to be raised."

Nevertheless, many young women, including Morsal, repeatedly reestablish contact with their families, despite warnings that they shouldn't. "They hope that their families will at some point accept their lifestyle," said the Papatya counselor. "But no one can force them to go somewhere they don't want to go or to leave the city. I can also understand these girls though because they are often very young and wouldn't want to just give everything up from one day to the next, either."

"They still want to be a part of things," says lawyer Ates. "Many have a very positive sense of the family which they have grown up with. At home they seek security and love. But reconciling a Western lifestyle with closeness to the family is a huge feat to accomplish." Morsal also knew that she was in danger—and she met with her brother and cousin anyway.

"I've been spending all of my time trying to imagine what was going through Ahmad's mind," Morsal's cousin told *Spiegel TV*. "I don't think much of him any more. And I very much hope that he will be given a just punishment. No matter what she did, Morsal didn't deserve this."

Kuwait's Culture Both Frees and Limits Women's Options

Haya Al-Mughni

Women's rights are often administered unevenly in Kuwait, claims Haya Al-Mughni in the following viewpoint. For example, men who kill their wives in "honor killings" receive reduced penalties. Women have many religious rights, but social norms and official policies continue to restrict women's freedom of movement Al-Mughni asserts. Sunni Family Law impacts the majority of Kuwaiti women, she says, giving men control over women. Freedom House, a nonprofit, nonpartisan organization that works to advance political and economic freedom, conducted this study of Kuwait, one of seventeen countries selected for the analysis. Al-Mughni is a Kuwaiti sociologist and the author of Women in Kuwait: The Politics of Gender.

As you read, consider the following questions:

1. In what year did Kuwait ratify the UN Convention on the Elimination of All Forms of Discrimination Against Women (CEDAW)?

2. What does Article 15 of the Passport Law state about a woman's ability to apply for a passport?

3. What is the minimum legal age for marriage for boys and girls in Kuwait, according to Haya Al-Mughni?

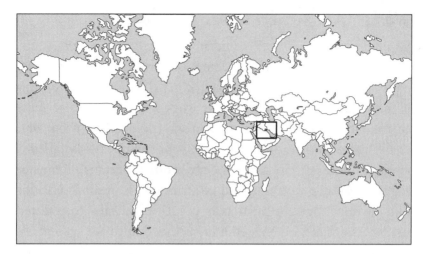

Adult women are recognized as full persons before the court and are not barred from testifying in the secular courts [in Kuwait]. However, Shari'a law, which is interpreted in family court, deems the testimony of one man to be equal to that of two women.

In most cases, women are treated equally under Kuwait's penal code and criminal laws. In principle, all perpetrators of murder, rape, or violence against women are subject to severe penalties such as life imprisonment or execution. However, in cases of "honor killings," the penalties are reduced for men. According to Article 153 of the penal code 16/1960, a husband who murders his wife and/or her partner during an adulterous act will be sentenced to a maximum of three years in jail.

"In most cases, women are treated equally under Kuwait's penal code and criminal laws."

While Kuwait practices the death penalty, death sentences are not carried out on pregnant women or mothers of dependent children. Women are housed in a separate prison from men, and those who are pregnant are exempted from prison work and receive special care in terms of food and rest.

Women Are Subject to Arbitrary Arrest

Women continue to suffer instances of gender-based and discriminatory arbitrary arrest, detention, and exile. Non-Kuwaiti nationals, men and women, may be expelled from the country if they are unable to renew their work and residence permits. In the late 1990s, following Islamists' (political activists who cite religion as their authority) pressure to increase social control and moral discipline in society, women became victims of harassment and were arrested at checkpoints. Sexual relations outside marriage, in particular prostitution, are considered moral crimes. Those engaging in such activities are susceptible to arrest, and foreign women may face imprisonment and deportation.

In 1994, Kuwait ratified CEDAW [UN Convention on the Elimination of All Forms of Discrimination Against Women] but adopted reservations on articles dealing with citizenship and voting rights. Reservations were also adopted on articles that call for equal rights concerning guardianship and the adoption of children.

The Kuwaiti National Assembly's Human Rights Committee can receive individual rights complaints from women, as well as complaints from foreign women seeking justice for employment-related grievances. Yet, in general, women's rights groups and the Human Rights Committee have not effectively dealt with the issues of gender discrimination and women's unequal access to justice.

How Women Can Achieve More Equality

1. The government should amend national laws in order to bring all legislation in conformity with the principles of nondiscrimination established in the constitution.

2. The government should amend the Kuwait Nationality Act of 1959 (specifically Article 2) to ensure that Ku-

waiti women have the same rights as Kuwaiti men to transfer nationality to foreign-born spouses and children.

3. The government should remove all reservations to CEDAW and take steps to implement it locally by bringing national laws in conformity with CEDAW.

"By custom, Kuwaiti women must request permission from their male guardians or parents to travel abroad or visit friends at night."

Kuwaiti Women Have Many Religious Rights

Women in Kuwait have few restrictions on the right to practice their religion and beliefs. Since the 1980s, religious observance among women has been on the rise. An increasing number of Kuwaiti women are now choosing to wear the *hijah*, pray in the mosques, and perform the pilgrimage rituals. Non-Muslim women also have the freedom to practice their religions. There are seven churches in Kuwait that serve the needs of the Christian community: Roman Catholic, Anglican, Greek Orthodox, Armenian Orthodox, Coptic Orthodox, Greek Catholic, and National Evangelical. Minority religious groups such as Sikhs, Hindus, Buddhists, and others are free to practice their religion in private homes or on the premises of the recognized churches.

Social norms and official policies remain a major hurdle to women's freedom of movement in Kuwait. By custom, Kuwaiti women must request permission from their male guardians or parents to travel abroad or visit friends at night. However, police generally do not arrest and return a woman to her home if she is found to be traveling alone. Under Article 15 of the Passport Law 11/1962, a married Kuwaiti woman cannot apply for a passport without the written approval of her husband, but an unmarried woman over 21 years of age can directly obtain her passport. However, many large businesses send their female employees abroad for business or conferences, and it is uncommon for women to face problems in their employment due to gender-related travel restrictions.

Sunni Family Law Affects the Majority

There are two different sets of active family laws in Kuwait: a Sunni Family Law, which was drawn up in accordance with the Maliki interpretation of Islam, and the Shi'a Family Law (the Jaafari laws). The Sunni Family Law affects the majority of Kuwaiti women, as Sunni Muslims constitute the majority of the population.

The Sunni Family Law, as interpreted in Kuwait, legitimizes male control over women. However, while Sunni Family Law requires husbands to support their wives and children, it does not provide the husband with the absolute right to *ta'a* (obedience). Article 89 of the Sunni Family Law specifies that a husband should not forbid his wife from working outside the home unless the work negatively affects "family interests." But the law does not clearly define family interests. The phrase can thus be interpreted as referring to the stability of the marriage or the upbringing of the children. The very notion that women have a right to work has been stigmatized by a commonly held view in Kuwait that women's neglect of domestic duties has led to a rise in divorce rates, juvenile delinquency, and drug addiction among Kuwaiti youth.

Unequal Rights to Marriage and Divorce

A husband is permitted to have more than one wife under both Sunni and Shi'a family laws. A man can marry a second wife without the permission of his first wife, and in some cases, without her knowledge. A wife may not petition for divorce on the grounds that her husband has taken another wife. If a man remarries, his second wife is expected to share the same house with his first wife, unless the husband has the means to provide his second wife with a new home. Under Sunni Family Law, a divorced woman will retain custody of her children until her sons reach 15 years of age and her daughters are married. If the mother remarries, she forfeits the right to custody.

While Sunni Family Law in Kuwait provides husbands with the unconditional right of divorce, women do not have the same rights and are unable to petition for divorce. However, women do have some form of protection against arbitrary divorce and mistreatment. A woman is owed financial compensation equal to one year of maintenance if her husband divorces her without her consent. Women also have the right to seek divorce if they are deserted in the marriage or subjected to *darar* (violent treatment that leads to physical injury). However, proof of injury is required in such cases. This is often difficult for many women, because they tend not to file complaints with the police and do not report causes of injury to doctors. Unsupportive and untrained police and doctors who examine abuse cases also hinder the gathering of evidence. According to reports, some husbands even try to bribe police to ignore charges of domestic violence.

Women Must Have Family Approval to Marry

The most discriminatory aspect of the Sunni Family Law in Kuwait involves the marriage rights of women. The Sunni Family Law deprives a woman of the right to conclude a marriage contract without the presence and consent of her *wali* (guardian). The wali is usually the woman's father, or in his absence, her brother, uncle, or other close male relative. In other words, a woman cannot marry the partner of her choice without the prior approval of her family. Yet, in cases in which the father of a Kuwaiti woman has refused her choice of hus-

Faiths Represented in Kuwait

Religions	Percent of Population
Sunni Islam	58.0
Shi'a Islam	33.0
Roman Catholic	6.5
Protestant	2.0
Melkite Greek Catholic	0.5
Syrian Catholic	<0.1
Bahá'í	0.2
Hinduism	0.2

Tore Kjeilen, "Religions: Kuwait,"
LookLex Encyclopedia, *2009.*

band, the Sunni Family Law grants a woman the right to appeal the decision of her wali in family court.

Some women opt to marry outside Kuwait to circumvent the marriage restrictions. Nevertheless, a marriage contracted outside Kuwait is not legally recognized within the country; the head of the bride's family has the right to ask the court to annul the marriage. The minimum legal age for marriage is 15 for girls and 17 for boys. Within the urban community, it is rare for girls to be married at an early age or forced into marriage. However, arranged marriages between families of similar social standings are still the norm. A woman can refuse to marry altogether and remain single, but the social burden placed on aging single women is so high that most women prefer an unhappy marriage to facing the social stigma of the spinster label.

Kuwait's penal code prohibits the practice of all forms of slavery, torture, cruelty, or degrading punishments against any person regardless of age, gender, religion, or nationality.

Slavery-like practices such as forced marriages and forbidding a person to leave the home are rarely reported. There are no forms of protection against these practices.

Domestic Workers Are Often Abused

Kuwait's labor laws specify that a working day should be restricted to eight hours, yet female domestic workers are often underpaid and forced to endure long working hours. Employers have been known to confiscate the passports of domestic workers, making it difficult for them to leave their jobs and/or the country. There are also reports of abuse of domestic workers and foreign women in the workplace.

Domestic workers can take legal recourse against their employers by filing complaints directly with the Dasma police station—the main center for dealing with employer abuse cases, or with Kuwait's administrative courts. Kuwait has been drafting a new labor law to protect the rights of domestic workers. Yet by the end of 2003, the law had not been finalized.

"Employers have been known to confiscate the passports of domestic workers, making it difficult for them to leave their jobs and/or the country."

While domestic violence is a concern in Kuwait, the lack of comprehensive data and research on this issue makes it difficult to assess the severity of the problem. No known NGO [nongovernmental organization] or government office efficiently works to collect such statistics. The scarcity of analyzed data on domestic violence in Kuwait is partly due to the social belief that this issue is a family affair. Victims of abuse are often reluctant to file complaints with the police due to fear and shame, and little effort has gone into providing assistance or protection to the victims. There are no laws against domestic violence, and there are no shelters, support centers, or free legal services to aid female victims.

Rape and sexual assault outside marriage tend to receive more attention from the police and the press than incidents of domestic violence. There have been reports of the physical abuse of female detainees under police custody, but no monitoring mechanism is in place to record such violations on a regular basis. By law, anyone found guilty of sexual violence and/or rape may receive a jail sentence or the death penalty, depending on the severity of the case.

Women's groups have not been able to work effectively to promote and actualize women's rights surrounding autonomy and personal freedom in Kuwait. In 2003, issues of domestic violence and the exploitation of domestic workers did not feature highly in the campaigns of Kuwaiti women's rights groups and received only sporadic coverage in the press.

Kuwaiti women's groups did advocate for amendments to a number of articles that curtail women's rights within marriage, including the right to choose one's husband and an increase in the minimum age of marriage for girls.

How Marriage Laws Can Be Improved for Women

1. The government should amend the age of marriage laws to increase the minimum age of marriage to 18 years for both boys and girls.

2. The government should amend the marriage contract laws under the family law to allow Kuwaiti women over 18 the right to marry the partner of their choice.

3. The government should start gender-sensitive, women's rights–oriented training for police and/or hire female police officers to investigate cases of violence so that women will feel more comfortable when reporting incidents of abuse.

4. The government and women's rights organizations should also organize public awareness campaigns on the problems of domestic violence.

A New Afghan Law Reverses Progress on Rights for Women

Golnaz Esfandiari

A new law passed by the Afghanistan parliament threatened to roll back progress on women's rights, claims Golnaz Esfandiari in the following viewpoint. Among other provisions, the law permits marital rape and puts many decisions about a wife's activities in the hands of the husband, she asserts. The president tried to assuage critics by saying the translation of the law misinterpreted its meaning. Women's rights leaders say the law would set dangerous precedents for all Afghan women, even though it would apply only to Shi'ite Muslims. Critics say the law contradicts the nation's constitution and international human rights conventions. Radio Free Europe/Radio Liberty (RFE/RL), an independent news organization funded by U.S. Congress, reports news in twenty-eight languages in twenty countries where a free press is not allowed or is not fully implemented. Esfandiari is a correspondent in the central newsroom of Radio Free Europe/Radio Liberty. Her areas of expertise include human rights, Iran, and media freedom.

As you read, consider the following questions:

1. In Golnaz Esfandiari's estimation, what percentage of Afghans are Shi'ite Muslims?

Golnaz Esfandiari, "New Law Seen as Setback for Afghan Women's Rights," Radio Free Europe/Radio Liberty, April 4, 2009. Copyright © 2009 RFE/RL, Inc. Reprinted with the permission of Radio Free Europe/Radio Liberty, 1201 Connecticut Ave., N.W. Washington DC 20036. www.rferl.org.

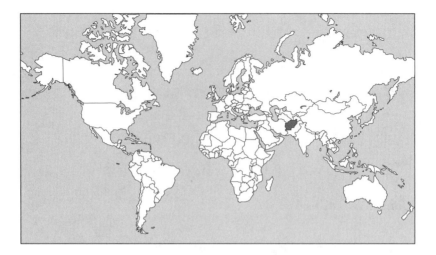

2. In what year did the Taliban fall in Afghanistan?

3. With whom did the Finnish foreign minister discuss the new law in The Hague?

A new law that applies only to Shi'ite Muslims in Afghanistan threatens to reintroduce some Taliban-era restrictions and reverse progress on women's rights in a country still struggling to recover from years of oppressive rule.

The law, which has not yet been published, was passed by parliament and was reportedly signed by President Hamid Karzai earlier this month [April 2009].

According to the United Nations High Commissioner for Human Rights, the legislation says that Afghan Shi'ite women will not have the right to leave their homes except for "legitimate" purposes, and forbids women from working or receiving education without their husbands' express permission.

The legislation explicitly permits marital rape by saying that a wife is bound to give a positive response to the sexual desires of her husband. It reportedly diminishes the right of mothers to be their children's guardians in the event of a divorce. And it makes it impossible for wives to inherit houses and land from their husbands—even though husbands may inherit property from their wives.

The legislation only applies to Shi'a, whom the Afghan Constitution allows to be governed by separate law where family issues are concerned. Shi'ite Muslims make up over 10 percent of Afghanistan's population.

The President Tries to Soothe Critics as He Reverses Progress

President Hamid Karzai sought to quell UN [United Nations] and Western alarm over the legislation, saying on April 4 [2009] that "we understand the concerns of our allies in the international community," according to Reuters [new service].

"Those concerns may be out of an inappropriate or not so good translation of the law or a misinterpretation of this," Karzai said. He suggested that a copy he'd seen did not merit such international criticism, and said the country's justice minister would study the law "very, very carefully" and then speak in detail about it on April 5 [2009].

"Since the fall of the Taliban ..., women in Afghanistan have seen their situation improve slowly but surely with the return of basic rights, such as the right to study and work."

"If there is anything that is of concern to us, then we will definitely take action in consultation with our ulema [or ulama; senior clerics] and send it back to the parliament," Karzai said, according to Reuters. "This is something we are serious about."

Since the fall of the Taliban in 2001, women in Afghanistan have seen their situation improve slowly but surely with the return of basic rights, such as the right to study and work.

But the new legislation threatens to turn back the clock. The UN High Commissioner for Human Rights, Navi Pillay, has called on President Hamid Karzai to rescind the law, saying that it is reminiscent of the decrees passed by the Taliban in the 1990s.

Sam Zarifi, Amnesty International's Asia-Pacific director, also had harsh words for the new legislation. "When we talk to ordinary people in Afghanistan, they all express concern about a return of the Taliban and Taliban laws," Zarifi said. "Now we see that even though the Taliban have not been able to come and capture Kabul, those who think like them bring these laws to Afghanistan from the back door."

Soraya Sobhrang, the head of the women's rights department of Afghanistan Independent Human Rights Commission [AIHRC], tells RFE/RL [Radio Free Europe/Radio Liberty] that the implementation of the law would set a disastrous precedent for all Afghan women.

"We are concerned that now that the law has been approved, all forms of violence against women and the discrimination that exists against women in Afghanistan become legal," Sobhrang said. "We are worried that similar laws, including the family law for Sunnis, could meet the same fate," and see a rollback of women's rights, she said.

Sobhrang said the international community should use its influence to change the law.

The Law Was Rushed Through Afghan Parliament

Reports say that Karzai initially signed the law under pressure from influential Shi'ite clerics in order to secure the vote of the Hazaras, a major and predominantly Shi'ite ethnic group in Afghanistan, in the upcoming presidential election.

Sabrina Saqib, an Afghan parliamentarian, told RFE/RL's Radio Free Afghanistan that the legislation was passed hastily in an effort to address religious sensitivities. She said the various articles of the law were not even read aloud, as is standard practice in parliament.

Iraqi Women Propose Their Own Constitutional Revision

Hanaa Edwar is a leader of the Iraqi Women's Movement.... She is campaigning against Article 41, a provision buried in the text of the draft constitution that places personal status laws under the influence of religion, sect, or belief. These are the laws that administer marriage, divorce, inheritance, child custody, and how religious courts settle disputes among Muslims, Christians, and Jews....

The ... movement has submitted its own language ... to replace the objectionable Article 41. It says that "the Iraqi state should ensure that personal status laws should be organized according to law." Edwar said they were often met with support for the movement's appeal but that "women's issues are one of the compromise issues among politicians."

Ellen Massey,
"Iraqi Women Resist Return to Sectarian Laws,"
AntiWar.com, June 26, 2007. http://antiwar.com.

"The arguments were based on Shari'a and religious laws, and there are always disagreements on these issues among clerics, lawmakers, and politicians," Saqib said. "Unfortunately the sensitivities prevented us from studying the law article by article, and it was voted in as a package."

While rights activists and some lawmakers, including Saqib, say the law contradicts the Afghan Constitution and international human rights conventions, Shi'ite lawmakers who helped draft the law have defended it, saying it protects women's rights.

During a March 31 [2009] conference on Afghanistan held in The Hague, Finnish Foreign Minister Alexander Stubb mentioned the law in discussions with U.S. Secretary of State Hillary Clinton. Reports say Clinton later raised the issue during her private meeting with Karzai.

"You cannot expect a country to develop if half its population are underfed, undereducated, under cared for, oppressed, and left on the sidelines."

Clinton told reporters at the conference that women's rights are a core element of U.S. foreign policy.

"You cannot expect a country to develop if half its population are underfed, undereducated, under cared for, oppressed, and left on the sidelines," Clinton said. "And we believe strongly that that's not in the interest of Afghanistan or any country—and it's certainly not part of our foreign policy and our strategic review. So we will continue to work very hard on behalf of women and girls in Afghanistan and around the world."

The International Community Is Scrutinizing the New Law

British Defense Secretary John Hutton told BBC [British Broadcasting Corporation] on the sidelines of the NATO [North Atlantic Treaty Organization] summit on April 4 [2009] that the issue "is going to be raised at the very highest level [of the Afghan government], I can assure you of that."

"The government of Afghanistan must abide by international agreements that it has entered into willingly," Hutton added.

Also in Strasbourg, Canadian Foreign Minister Lawrence Cannon said the law as described would be "alarming and troubling for many allies," and urged Karzai to explain the legislation.

Israel Sees a Revival of Women's Prayer Books

Sybil Sheridan

In the following viewpoint, Sybil Sheridan reviews Aliza Lavie's book, published in Israel, on the history of Jewish women's prayers. Sheridan notes that Lavie focuses primarily on the two historical bodies of prayers for women, the Yiddish tehinnot and the Italian prayer books. Some of the prayers have been translated into Hebrew with an accompanying commentary in Hebrew. Examples have been taken from seven different areas of women's lives. Examples of women's prayers from recent decades have also been included. Lavie's book continues the study of women's prayers in the tehinnot that has been going on for the last twenty years. Sybil Sheridan is the editor of Hear Our Voice: Women Rabbis Tell Their Stories.

As you read, consider the following questions:

1. Who were the authors of the tehinnot or devotional literature for women, according to Kohler and Eisenstein?
2. What is the difference in the way that male and female prayers were transmitted from generation to generation?
3. What are the seven different areas of women's lives, according to Sheridan?

Sybil Sheridan, "Aliza Lavie—*Tefillat Nashim: Jewish Women's Prayers Throughout the Ages*," *Nashim: A Journal of Jewish Women's Studies and Gender Issues*, vol. 15, 2008, pp. 212ff. Copyright © 2008 Indiana University Press. Reproduced by permission.

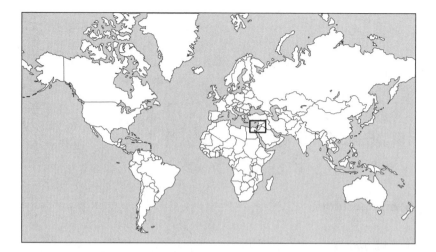

The entry "Devotional Literature" by Kaufmann Kohler and Judah David Eisenstein in the 1905 Jewish Encyclopedia contains a section on Yiddish Tehinnot—devotional literature for women—in which we read the following comments:

> The names of the authors are nearly all fictitious and high sounding and have been affixed to make the tehinnot salable. It is known that some of the tehinnot were written by indigent students of the Rabbinical Seminary of Wilna or Jitomir ... for nominal sums, and that the publishers stipulated that the writers should fashion the composition in tearful and heartrending phrases to suit the taste of the women readers. This forced cultivation of devotional feeling rendered the tehinnot exaggerated and over-colored, and this did not escape the criticism and ridicule of the men against the women who were such devotees of the tehinnot. (IV, p. 551; online at www. jewishencyclopedia. com)

Kohler and Eisenstein thus dismissed not only the tehinnot, but also women and their prayer life. There is no suggestion in the entry that women might themselves be authors of prayers, or that they could exercise choice or discrimination in the prayers they offered. The implication is that they were ignorant and taken in by the devotional equivalent of a cheap novel, written purely for profit.

A century on, and a very different attitude to these prayers has emerged. Much has been written about the tehinnot in the last twenty years, and Aliza Lavie follows the now generally accepted view that many of them were written by women, and that, in the main, they were carefully composed to meet specific needs. Further examples of women's prayers are drawn from surviving Italian prayer books, hand written and lovingly prepared, often by fathers for their daughters or husbands for their wives. Yet others are individual prayers—some written by women, and some by men for women—from different places around the Jewish world, meeting women's devotional needs in a variety of contexts and occasions. While not all of them may excel in literary merit (though since many have been translated into Hebrew from other languages, it is difficult to tell), Lavie, by placing them in their historical context—her notes appear alongside each prayer–renders them inspirational and exceedingly moving. No one, reading this book could make fun of a woman's choice of prayer.

"The authors of many of the prayers from eastern Europe seem to have been pious but poorly educated, while those from central and western Europe were far better able to express themselves and make sophisticated use of Hebrew and biblical allusions."

Full of variety in subject, mood and style, the book is attractively set in two colors, distinguishing prayer from commentary, with a stylized decoration around each title . . . the texts are expected to be prayed rather than studied. On the whole, these are prayers that once were alive in the supplications of the petitioner. Is it possible that they will live again on the lips of our own generation? The success with which

Tefillat nashim has been met since its publication two years ago suggests that this is happening.

Aliza Lavie's task has been a difficult one. Throughout Jewish history, a man's strict daily recitation of the statutory prayers took place in the public arena of the synagogue. These were the prayers that were written down and preserved in siddurim over the ages. Women's prayer, on the other hand, was a private matter and on the whole extemporary. Prayers were transmitted orally from mother to daughter—an oral tradition that, with the vicissitudes of the twentieth century, has been all but lost. In addition, male scholars' disinterest in the subject gave rise to the suggestion that women did not pray. It has taken a generation of female scholars to show this to be quite wrong, and to revisit such ancient prayers as do exist in writing and reevaluate them in the context of the ages in which they were written.

While many studies have been done on individuals and on specific groups of prayers, Lavie's book, to my knowledge, is the first to have gathered examples of all the known literature relating to women's prayer life and rituals. This impressive collection covers seven different areas of women's lives: daily life; infertility and fertility; motherhood; the three "women's" mitzvot of candle-lighting, separating hallah and family purity; festivals and special days; petitions in times of distress; and prayers for peace and redemption. The prayers range from medieval to modern times, and they come from east and west–from Kurdistan and Tunisia, from the anusim of Portugal and the inmates of Auschwitz. The styles vary, from straightforward outpourings of feeling to elaborately composed piyyutim (liturgical poems). The authors of many of the prayers from eastern Europe seem to have been pious but poorly educated, while those from central and western Europe were far better able to express themselves and make sophisticated use of Hebrew and biblical allusions. The latter are wonderful to read, but they sometimes lose the immediacy of the simpler, impassioned pleas.

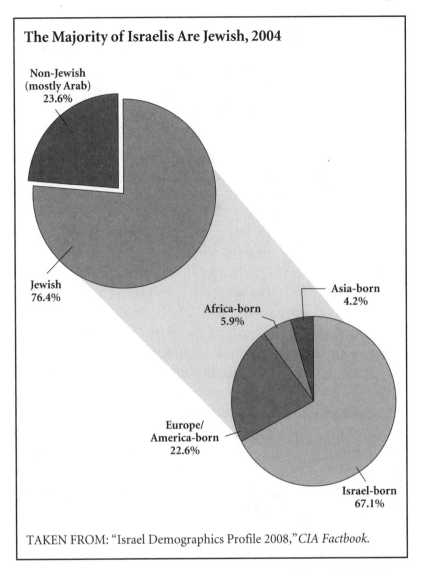

The Majority of Israelis Are Jewish, 2004

Non-Jewish
(mostly Arab)
23.6%

Jewish
76.4%

Africa-born
5.9%

Asia-born
4.2%

Europe/
America-born
22.6%

Israel-born
67.1%

TAKEN FROM: "Israel Demographics Profile 2008," *CIA Factbook.*

A significant portion of the Israeli population has European origins, and Lavie finds many of the prayers in her book authored by European Jewish women.

Tefillat nashim includes descriptions of women's practices as well as their prayers, and of songs and poetry that in all probability did not pertain to a ritual setting. All these, with the explanatory notes that accompany them, bring a sense that there is a long history to women's participation in the religious life of Judaism—a prayer life separate from that of the men, but vibrant and full of meaning.

I have no doubt that this was the case, but the book also demonstrates how little has survived. There is hardly anything from before the sixteenth century. The clearly extensive research that Lavie carried out focused largely on the only two historical bodies of prayers for women known today—the Yiddish tehinnot and the Italian prayer books. There are also prayers by individuals, such as Fanny Neuda in the nineteenth century, whose output was prolific. There are a few named women and men of earlier generations and a very few women of more recent times, remembering the prayers or customs of their grandmothers. The scantiness of this last group only attests to how much has been lost. The book also includes some recorded observations, such as those by the fifteenth-century Mishnah commentator Ovadia of Bartinoro of women's practices in Sicily, and a record, sadly not referenced, of women's custom of saying the prayer nishmat kolhai during pregnancy. These descriptions are fascinating, but there are not many of them, again suggesting that, simply, not enough is known about women's prayer life and rituals of the past to fully round out the picture. It is surely stretching a point to include Ya commimos, a Ladino version of Birkat hamazon (the Grace after Meals), as a women's prayer, on the grounds that it was recited by those who were not familiar with the traditional Hebrew version; there were plenty of men in the same situation who sang it, too.

Finally, there are rituals and prayers of much more recent vintage. Given the huge number of prayers devised in the last few decades, I would have liked to know how Lavie made her choices, but it is fascinating to see how well these newer prayers fit into the general pattern. In fact, the origins of some of the prayers held a few surprises. The prayer of a divorced woman turned out to be from the nineteenth century, while that to be said at Rachel's tomb appears to be modern. A prayer to find a partner (as is surely said by any woman out speed dating) was written by Rabbi Nahman of Bratzlav. Perhaps this shows the agelessness of the topic. In 1445 or 2005, the hopes, fears and yearnings remain the same.

As a rabbi in a congregation, I am always on the lookout for new prayers to be used in specific situations. Many of those included in *Tefillat nashim* would fit into the lifecycle rituals that are being created and developed to meet the needs of individual women today. Some prayers might also be used with benot mitvah as a way of explaining Jewish women's spirituality in past ages to them, and encouraging them to explore their own. By writing their own prayers, they, too, can contribute to the long tradition attested in this book

What is clear is that this can only be a beginning. As women today continue to compose rituals to meet our increasingly complicated needs, it is to be hoped that Aliza Lavie will continue her work of collecting and collating extant material lying forgotten in libraries, and bringing it all to our attention.

Saudi Arabian Women Hope for Greater Religious Tolerance

Basma Al-Mutlaq

In the following viewpoint, Basma Al-Mutlaq asserts that a recent government change in leadership has lifted the hopes of Saudi Arabian women that they will be more included in the government and have more educational opportunities. While men still predominate in positions of power, she claims, the appointment of young, educated men signifies a desire to change many long-held beliefs and customs that resulted in diminishing social and economic status for women. Arab News is an English language daily newspaper that aims to break barriers between Arabs and non-Arabs by providing information for diverse cultural communities. Al-Mutlaq holds a PhD in comparative and feminist literature of the Middle East from the School of Oriental and African Studies, London University. She is an analyst with the gender statistics unit of Jordan's Department of Statistics.

As you read, consider the following questions:

1. What label does extremism often use to describe those who disagree with its tenets, according to Basma Al-Mutlaq?

2. What cliché term do Saudi men use in describing how women should be protected, in the author's observation?

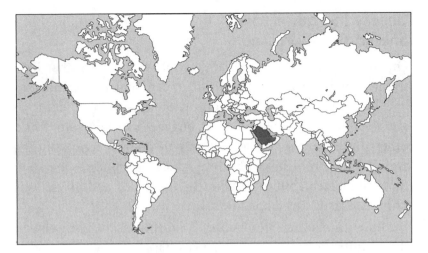

3. What right does Al-Mutlaq identify as a necessary characteristic for an equal partner in a globalized economy?

The significant government reshuffle we recently witnessed in the Kingdom [of Saudi Arabia] suggests a willingness to effect change in an institution that has hitherto excluded women on the grounds of religious and cultural customs. The scales are still heavily weighted in favor of the male subject; nevertheless it is a long-anticipated development that is welcomed by women here.

For those generations who have known nothing but exclusion and gender apartheid, and have suffered an acute sense of alienation from their own society in the past, it means a new leaning toward the integration of all subjects, regardless of gender. This may seem a utopian dream, but the hope that we are at least moving in the direction of tolerance of the other and openness toward different ideas, should motivate us to press for further positive steps. Extremism of any kind has proven over and again to be a perilous path that leads not only to horrific violence, and hatred and intolerance for the "other," but also intimidates those who at present are finding it difficult to integrate into a hostile environment.

Deeply Ingrained Ideas
Should Be Addressed

On the subject of "hope", many people are hopeful that having a woman in government will mean that the authorities will start an in-depth discussion on the quality of teaching in girls' schools and colleges, and engage with educators and other professionals on the best way to address long-standing and chronic problems within the education system—a system that fails lamentably to respond to the needs and aspirations of half of its young population.

As enthralled and excited as I [am] and everyone else in this country is to see these changes happening, I believe that women need and deserve more than one representative in government to address pressing issues—issues that are at heart cultural. Deeply ingrained in the mentality of people and in the fabric of this society are ideas and assumptions that give the male the lead over women, and the right to control the physical and intellectual dimensions of her life.

The appointment of young, educated men to positions within the new government signifies a desire for renewal and a determination to defy some of the prevalent medieval elements that persist at the highest levels. These elements have for too long promoted toxic ideas about women that have resulted in a shameful deterioration of women's overall social and economic status in a country that prides itself on its wealth creation and technological progress.

I am surely not the only one who is tired of these clichés about women, whereby they are not independent human beings full of dynamism and ideas, but are "pearls in a shell" that should be protected and taken care of. Even more insulting is the idea that "women are mentally and religiously incompetent"—yet another false pretext for giving men the upper hand in their relations with women. These interpretations of religious traditions not only result in segregation of, and the imposition of rigid boundaries between the sexes, but

Saudi Arabian Women Are Fulfilling Their Right to Education

The Saudi government has prioritised providing free education to all citizens without any discrimination, making education compulsory for children between the ages of 6 and 15. . . .

The government has also made considerable efforts to promote gender equality, and to ensure girls equal access to basic education. In September 2000, it signed and ratified the [UN] Convention on the Elimination of All Forms of Discrimination Against Women (CEDAW) with some reservations.

National results also indicate there has been considerable progress in achieving gender equality among students; the number of female students at all school levels from 270,000 in 1974–75 increased to more than 2 million in 2004–05. . . .

Currently, more than 38 educational institutes exist for women in the country alongside eight universities under the patronage of the Ministry of Education and women represent more than 58% of the total number of Saudi university students. The total number of female students enrolled seeking a bachelor's degree more than tripled between 1995–96 and 2005–06 to more than 340,000.

Rana Mesbah,
"Women's Education in Saudi Arabia: The Way Forward,"
AME Info, June 9, 2009. www.ameinfo.com.

stipulate that it is a rule of faith that should be enforced with often brutal policing methods. This is a major obstacle to the achievement of equality in the workplace for educated women, who still find themselves left out in the cold, and must experience the disappointment of seeing less able men reach the top of their careers. The fact that people in this country are rewarded positions and salaries on the basis of their gender, not of their qualifications or ability, makes it difficult to argue that women are not discriminated against in the job market. Indeed, if one wants to talk about competence, then we must question the wisdom of appointing an incompetent man over a competent woman because of some misguided notion that one sex is innately capable.

"The appointment of young, educated men to positions within the new government signifies a desire for renewal and a determination to defy some of the prevalent medieval elements that persist at the highest levels."

Correcting the Imbalance of Power Is Overdue

I can only hope that we will have more women representatives in government in the near future, that women will be more visible in public, and that major restrictions on mobility will be lifted to give women the space and autonomy they need to recognize themselves as socially equal beings.

The imbalance of power between the sexes is a long overdue issue that should be promptly addressed in the newly assembled government; it cannot be overstated how important it is to have universal suffrage [voting rights] in a country that wants to see itself as an equal partner in a globalized economy. We might be a proud country, but we must ask ourselves whether this pride is justified as long as we humiliate and alienate 50 percent of our population.

Periodical Bibliography

The following articles have been selected to supplement the diverse views presented in this chapter.

Amal Mohammed Al-Malki	"Islamic Feminists Distinguish Islam from Muslims," *Common Ground News Service*, March 31, 2009. www.commongroundnews.org.
Associated Press	"Polygamy Law Taken to Court in British Columbia," October 22, 2009.
Compass Direct News	"Christian in Somalia Who Refused to Wear Veil Is Killed," October 27, 2009. www.compassdirect.org.
Earth Times	"Reconstructed Hymens Are Forbidden, Saudi Religious Scholars Say," November 5, 2009. www.earthtimes.org.
Economist	"Sudan's Dress-Code Row: A Martyr to Her Trousers," August 8, 2009.
Angelo Izama	"Uganda: Govt Attacks Catholic Church over Divorce," *Monitor*, October 7, 2009.
Peter Kenny	"In Sweden Lesbian Bishop Is Not a 'Hot Issue', in Africa, Church Fumes," *Ecumenical News International*, November 17, 2009.
Joseph Yun Li-sun	"To Stop Abortion, We Must Change Society, Korean Church Says," *AsiaNews*, November 17, 2009.
Nesrine Malik	"The Great Betrayal," *New Statesman*, August 13, 2009.
Martin Patriquin	"Critics Stoke Hijab Debate in Quebec," *Maclean's*, May 28, 2009.
Nicole Winfield	"African Nuns Tell Vatican They Want More Influence," *Associated Press*, October 9, 2009.

GLOBALVIEWPOINTS

CHAPTER 4

Women's Economic Rights

India Sees an Influx of Women in Engineering Careers

Pragya Singh

In Pragya Singh's view, women in India are entering the engineering profession in record numbers to take advantage of its stable career path and attractive salaries. Most opt for jobs in the service sector, including outsourcing, information technology, and retail, which are typically located in more urban areas than so-called mainstream engineering jobs, Singh claims. India's colleges and universities are offering curricula designed for female engineering students. Singh is a special correspondent for Outlook india.com.

As you read, consider the following questions:

1. As Pragya Singh reports, what percentage of engineering students in educational institutes were women in 2008?

2. According to Hitesh Oberoi, where are most of the industrial belts in India?

3. What is the salary range for engineering graduates in India, according to the author?

Journalism is what Shalini Babu had always wanted to do. But when it came to choosing a career after school, she opted for engineering. She completed a four-year engineering course from DMS College in Bangalore, and joined the city's

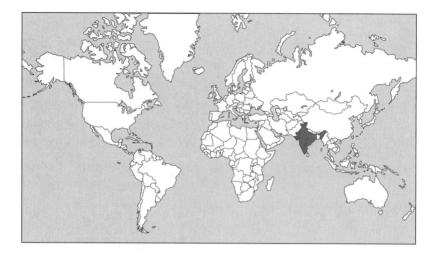

booming IT [information technology] industry in 2005. "I became an engineer for the standard reasons," says the 26-year-old. "It is a stable career option with good chances of rising up the ladder."

Derided long enough for not having a head for numbers and shying away from anything remotely technology-related, or dismissed as ultra 'studious' if they did make the cut, women are no longer an oddity in engineering institutes across the country. Confirmation comes from Vidya, all of 20, who says there are 25 other girls in her class of 60 at the S.P. [Sardar Patel] College, a private institution affiliated with the Mumbai University. All of a sudden, engineering institutions are witnessing an influx of women students like never before. The percentage of women students opting for engineering went up from 1 percent in 1975 to 10 percent in 1990, according to a 2001 study by IIT Mumbai. Cut to industry estimates in 2007, and you discover women are 23 percent of engineering graduates in India. Most institutes today [2008] say 10–25 percent of their students are women.

Ten out of 70 students in his last class were women, IIT Delhi professor Dr. Kiran Seth tells us. "In the last five years, there has been a surge in the number of women students in engineering," he says. "Few women were seen in the engineering classes of the '70s or '80s. They are now 30 percent of the class strength across streams." And far from being a 'subdued' lot in male-dominated classes, these women are confident and completely at ease.

"Derided long enough for not having a head for numbers and shying away from anything remotely technology-related, . . . women are no longer an oddity in engineering institutes across the country."

Women Are Attracted to Engineering Jobs in the Service Sector

But even as the number of women studying engineering is growing, unemployability hasn't kept pace. The IIT Mumbai 2001 study had noted that the percentage of unemployed women engineers had gone up from 20 percent in 1990 to 35 percent in 1998. Shedding some light on the issue, Hitesh Oberoi, COO [chief operating officer], Naukri.com, says, "The way India planned its economic development, most industrial belts were in rural areas. In our society, few women wanted to move to these places. That's why men led in mainstream engineering." But the advent of the service sector possibly changed all that. In a 2007 survey it conducted, Naukri found that 20 percent of its online job applicants were women but most of them were opting for jobs in outsourcing, information technology and the retail sector. "Women applicants for civil engineering positions are less than 10 percent," he says, though he adds that the number has grown in the recent past. "If businesses other than services show a similar growth trend, the demand for skills will pull more women toward the factory floor as well." Services opened up avenues for women engineers only about a decade ago, and manufacturing remains an as-yet untapped field. Once that sector embarks on realising their potential, opportunities for women engineers will only escalate.

According to Wing Commander Arvind K. Poothia, secretary and director general, Institution of . . . Engineers [India] (IEI), which promotes advancement of engineering in India, this is a big change from the past, when an engineering degree was a dead-end qualification for women. "India even has women marine engineers today—a tough and demanding career through which women are challenging the myth that they seek easy, deskbound careers," Poothia says. At the IEI's annual gathering of women-only engineers, attendance stood at 500 in 2007, up three times since 150 in 2001, he points out.

Educational Institutions Are Offering Women-Only Curricula

Educational institutions too are responding to the demand. Women-only engineering colleges and universities have mushroomed all across the country, be it the MKSS Cummins College of Engineering in Pune or the Idhaya Engineering College for Women in Hyderabad. However, Poothia cautions against the trend of getting a degree for the sake of a degree. "The quality of education is more important than the degree," he says. Thankfully, he adds, unlike men, women are not making career choices blindly. He could well be talking of Saima Mohan, a biomedical engineer who teaches at Bangalore's M.S. Ramaiah School of Advanced Studies and also conducts industry relevant research at the institute. "I am interested in research work," says Saima. "This is what I like to do. I'm not too focused on making money." The money isn't too bad either. Starting salaries for engineering graduates average Rs [rupees; Indian currency] 15,000 a month and go up to Rs 50,000 a month if one has a degree from one of the top 20 institutes.

And human resource [HR] experts have no complaints from women engineering employees. They tend to be more loyal, and are rarely known to switch jobs for higher salary alone. Make a workplace woman friendly and you can keep

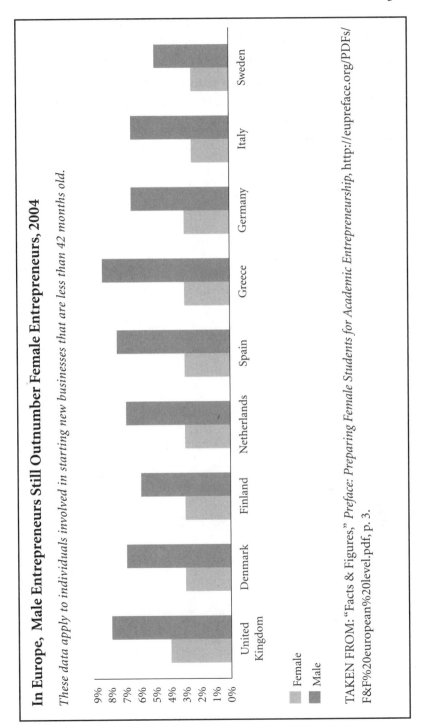

In Europe, Male Entrepreneurs Still Outnumber Female Entrepreneurs, 2004

These data apply to individuals involved in starting new businesses that are less than 42 months old.

TAKEN FROM: "Facts & Figures," *Preface: Preparing Female Students for Academic Entrepreneurship*, http://eupreface.org/PDFs/F&F%20european%20level.pdf, p. 3.

her for a long time. The service sector realised this quite early. "Now the crunch for talent is being felt across sectors. As a result, making the workplace woman friendly is no longer just a nice-to-do thing but a business imperative," says strategic HR consultant Hema Ravichandar. Hence crèches [nursery schools] in the office for working mothers or the option of working from home.

Cameroon's Female Farmers Unite in Grassroots Activism

Susan Diduk

Susan Diduk describes in the following viewpoint how rural Cameroonian women, many of whom are small landholder farmers called "grassfields women" and are past childbearing age, form groups that march and demonstrate to protest political and civil injustices. The women are often naked, a symbol of their mystical power and flaunting of societal norms. Diduk states that human and crop fertility are important interrelated themes in rural Cameroonian culture, so women play an important role in sustaining society. Diduk, an associate professor in the department of sociology/anthropology at Denison University, has performed research in Cameroon for many years. She often publishes articles on rural social activism.

As you read, consider the following questions:

1. What materials do the women marchers use in the necklaces they wear, according to Susan Diduk?
2. What is the word used to identify the male regulatory association that approves censure of men and women?
3. In what year did a Cameroonian photographer take photos of Takembeng women marchers?

Susan Diduk, "The Civility of Incivility: Grassroots Political Activism, Female Farmers, and the Cameroon State," *African Studies Review*, vol. 47, no. 2, September 2004, pp. 32–36. Copyright © 2004 African Studies Association. Reproduced by permission.

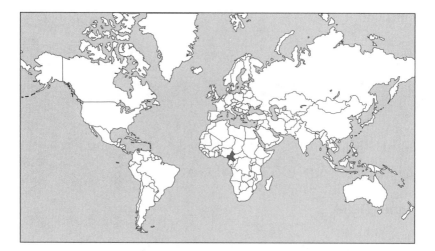

Political activism by female farmers is by no means new to the Northwest Province of Cameroon, nor is it amorphous.

Participants typically move in loosely structured groups of older women. Calls to congregate circulate informally by word of mouth over cooking fires, at farms, and on the roadways. It also spreads formally via members who are officially designated messengers; they notify women across particular quarters of a fondom. Before advancing along village paths or main roads within and between chiefdoms, women congregate in a prearranged location. They assemble in various guises; while old clothing is the norm, some women intentionally mix bright and often garish colors. Many wear necklaces made from old bottle tops or wild seeds taken from the bush. Stocking caps or, more recently, baseball caps that are sometimes worn backwards adorn heads. Others wear whistles around their necks and blow them to signal for assistance. When women march they sing; they ululate [howl or wail] loudly and can be heard long before they pass. A rich song repertoire serves as the collective memory of earlier mobilizations. Women may also "sing the name of" anyone suspected of venality or compromising community survival. Those "named" include individuals of local and national stature. The intent is to embarrass and shame them publicly. Statements by women that they are "driving hunger away," "holding the country," and that it is "a time for proper war" give expression to an activism that is couched in terms of defending community survival.

Women's Unorthodox Behavior Makes Viewers Uncomfortable

My experience is that women marching "to hold the country" enjoy themselves immensely. They are greatly amused by, and delight in telling about, their dereliction of duties when they abandon cooking pots and hungry husbands. Comedians among the activists are respected highly for their humor and skill at punning. Indeed, they often function as leaders. In Kedjom Keku they are called *vugweys* and are especially bold and shameless in mocking authority figures, using nakedness to their advantage and making rude and lewd comments about malefactors or teasing bystanders. There have been numerous occasions over the years when I have seen men as well as women visibly made uncomfortable by these women's vulgar jokes and accusations. Males are uniformly excluded from mobilizations, regardless of age, and women expect them to remain at a distance. It is quite common to observe men disappearing quickly down village paths or city streets to avoid such women. But men's abrupt departures are not simply the result of embarrassment; they describe a deep unease that originates in the ritually dangerous nature of women's actions.

These local traditions of protest and disciplinary action are institutionalized and deeply embedded in grassfields history.... Indeed, a brief discussion of that history and the cultural right of women to march is necessary to understand Takembeng's activism in the 1990s.[1] Throughout the precolo-

1. Takembeng refers to the political activism movement as well as the women who participate. They are typically older subsistence farming women who protest with apparently "uncivil" displays.

Shanghai Traditions Give Rise to Gender Equity in Australia

Migrants from China are a relatively recent migrant group to Australia. The sharp increase of Chinese population in Australia over the past two decades has drawn the attention of scholars from various fields. However, studies.... of gender relations among the group have remained largely unexamined.

Drawing on the frameworks of resource and power structure in the studies of gender relations, [a study in the *Journal of Men's Studies*] aims to examine the division of labor among recently arrived Chinese in Australia, with a focus on men's housework participation and regional differences if there are any and why....

A pattern of Shanghai men's housework involvement emerged, which shows that Shanghai men are not only intensively but also voluntarily involved in housework. Also salient is Shanghai men's self-identification as being a Shanghai man that links to their perceived gender roles in the family. The observed pattern of Shanghai men's behaviors differs from what most would consider traditional men's roles. This phenomenon, Shanghai men's intense involvement in housework, cannot be explained simply by the resource/power structure framework.... Evidence yielded in this study indicates that there is a regional tradition in men's housework participation that goes back to the migrants' home origin of Shanghai. It has associations with social policy, gender ideology, and practices in China at large. It also relates to the given context of Shanghai, its early industrial history, women's massive participation in the workforce, and early exposure to Western influences.

Wei Wei Da, "A Regional Tradition of Gender Equity: Shanghai Men in Sydney, Australia," Journal of Men's Studies, vol. 12, no. 2, Winter 2004, pp. 136 and 146.

nial and colonial eras, and still today, rural women regularly joined together to censure men as well as other women. These actions, referred to as *keluh* in the fondom of Kedjom Keku, where I have done research since 1981, are parallel to and approved by the male regulatory association, *kwyfon*. Women had the right—especially in the quarter where they lived—to discipline men and women accused of witchcraft, theft, or the abuse of minors or the elderly. They could punish those who engaged in behaviors that insulted womanhood or other offenses against the moral order, such as the beating of a pregnant woman, incest, or excessive and unprovoked beating of a wife, daughter, or son.

The actions of keluh were in defense of community norms and morality, rather than simply protest against transgressions. The goal was to stop unethical behavior and to obtain restitution and reconciliation. . . .

"Throughout the precolonial and colonial eras, and still today, rural women regularly joined together to censure men as well as other women."

Women's Marches Follow a Distinct Set of Customs

When rural women march and demonstrate in Bamenda, they are almost always referred to as "Takembeng." These contemporary women's marches follow a clear social pattern, with a well-recognized cultural iconography. Marchers are older women, although in my experience premenopausal and middle-aged women also participate. Many are poor, with little or no formal education, and most women also take part in mobilizations in their home communities. Today [around 2004] they move in tight groups of about thirty to several hundred at a time. Old clothing of the sort women wear at the farm is most customary: a faded wrapper, a torn shirt or blouse, and a worn pair of plastic sandals or flip-flops. Some marchers carry sticks they raise intermittently, as though they were guns. Others walk with dried grass tied in knots, probably *nchogee*, a medicine of protection. As I suggested earlier, some wear hats or more eccentric clothing, like mismatched or incongruous combinations of brightly colored clothing meant to be humorous. If they come from far away, many carry shoulder bags containing food and water. During the 1990s, in order to avoid being recognized and intercepted by government security forces as they walked from rural areas to urban centers (some traveling as much as forty miles), some women wore better clothing and moved in small groups of five or six. This political strategy allowed them to go unnoticed until they had congregated in large groups in urban centers.

In general, they are immediately recognized by urbanites, whether people approve of Takembeng's actions or not. This is no surprise, because ordinarily when women take to the roadways they move independently and are [loath] to interact or to talk with others (reminiscent of local priestly societies going about their ritual duties). A vivid example of Takembeng activity occurred in the antigovernment marches on the streets of Bamenda throughout the 1990s. If Takembeng participated, they were always the first to march, with other marchers following at a marked distance of at least three to four hundred yards. One woman carried a small clay pot said to contain protective medicine guarding against misfortune and illness. (Let me note here that it is quite common generally for people who travel outside of their natal rural communities to fortify themselves medically against a "dangerous world.") Fellow marchers also carried stalks of the *nkung* plant, which features prominently in grassfields rites of renewal, restoration, and fertility.

Takembeng Women Are Reputed to Have Spiritual Powers

Even though men were much more numerous in the marches, the pronounced gap between Takembeng and other marchers—whether younger women or men of all ages—was an expression of Takembeng's spiritual powers. Their difference in demeanor was equally telling. Photographs taken in 1993 by a professional Cameroonian photographer show Takembeng women looking very serious, and the roadway where they are marching completely absent of onlookers. Behind them at a far distance are the swelling crowds of protestors overflowing commercial thoroughfares. Juxtaposed to the somber and stern Takembeng marchers, other protestors are gesticulating, yelling, and exuberant.

"These movements ... affirm existing political and religious institutions, celebrate women's spiritual authority, and assert their moral obligation to act on behalf of community welfare."

The expressive form of these marches replicates that of keluh and fombuen in rural villages. Again, when women "come out" people self-consciously and rapidly move away. Onlookers may literally stop in their tracks and turn their backs to the women, scuttle into open doorways, or dive down side paths. Children are shooed away and personal conversations left unfinished. The reality is that people do look, but from a distance and surreptitiously. The fact that marchers sometimes move in complete silence (again, like men in priestly and medicinal societies) adds to the unease. One senses keenly that people are uncomfortable and would prefer to be elsewhere. Yet later in conversation, observers often say it is risky, even dangerous, to watch such women. When Takembeng march in town, there are many accounts of men becoming very ill, even dying, because they "saw" them. And the danger is always said to involve seeing women naked or in various stages of undress. . . .

Women Behave in Culturally Legitimate Ways

These movements [do not] simply resist structures of authority or protest against the supposedly marginal position of women. As with keluh and fombuen, they affirm existing political and religious institutions, celebrate women's spiritual authority, and assert their moral obligation to act on behalf of community welfare. Theirs is a history of acting within the system, as guardians of communal morality, not necessarily protesting outside of it, or being subordinate to it. This helps to explain why women engage in actions that may seem "disgusting" from the viewpoint of each of these societies, yet are deeply conventional. Again, far from being "uncivil," there is a culturally legitimate etiquette when women walk naked or engage in other apparently scatological acts.

Added evidence that there is a civility to what otherwise would be shocking and egregious is that not all women engage in such acts. As I have said, it is only postmenopausal women who expose their sexual organs, defecate, urinate, and so on. Because they are beyond childbearing, such actions are no longer threatening to their own fertility. Interestingly enough, Takembeng women take great care to shield younger women from such actions, moving them some distance away from their naked "mothers." Finally, even women who do participate in such actions do not do so lightly. Many of the women are Christian and have come to accept more European principles of modesty—for example, the ubiquitous use of bras. Thus they may consider going naked to be immodest. Yet their awareness of the power of nakedness as an act of moral censure and outrage outweighs their momentary embarrassment.

In the Post-Socialist Transition in Russia, Women Entered Employment More Readily, but into Lower-Paying Jobs

Theodore P. Gerber and Olga Mayorova

The Soviet-era gender pay gap was similar to that in Western capitalist countries. The centralized determination of wages left little room for discrimination in wage on the basis of gender. However, when this centralized economic force was removed in post-Soviet Russia, employers were more free to discriminate. Women were paid less and channeled into lower-quality jobs. However, the lower pay for women tended to make them more attractive to employers, so that women tended to enter employment more easily than men. Employers restructured their work around professions dominated by women to take advantage of the lower cost of employing women. Theodore P. Gerber is a Professor of Sociology at the University of Wisconsin-Madison. Olga Mayorova is Postdoctoral Research Associate at the University of Arizona.

As you read, consider the following questions:

1. According to Gerber and Mayorova, what percentage of men's wages did women earn in Soviet Russia?

Theodore P. Gerber and Olga Mayorova, "Dynamic Gender Differences in a Post-Socialist Labor Market: Russia, 1991–1997," *Social Forces*, vol. 84, no. 4, June 2006, pp. 2047ff. Copyright © 2006 University of North Carolina Press. Used by permission.

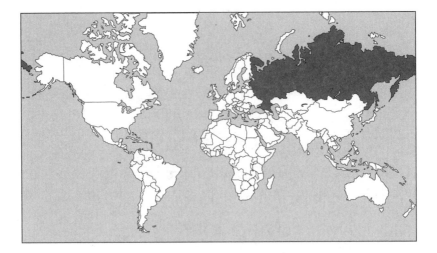

2. What do Gerber and Mayorova conclude about the relative productivity of Russian men and women during the economic transition?

3. How did women with college degrees fare early in the transition? To what do Gerber and Mayorova attribute that pattern?

How does the shift from state socialism affect gender inequality in the labor market? Many predicted that surging unemployment and the reallocation of jobs across economic branches and sectors would hurt women disproportionately. Others argued that market reforms would benefit women. Most studies addressing this question analyze gender wage gaps with cross-sectional data. We advance the debate by examining how gender differences in rates of labor market transitions (entry to or exit from employment, job mobility) and in the quality of new jobs change over time. We analyze employment histories spanning 1991–1997 from a representative sample of 3,580 Russians. . . .

Women are disadvantaged on the labor market to the extent that, relative to men, they have higher rates of layoff and voluntary employment exit, lower rates of employment entry and job mobility, higher odds that their new jobs are low-quality positions, and lower odds that they are high-quality. . . . We compare gross and net effects to see if observable human capital and structural location in the labor market produce gender inequality. We find gross and net gender effects of similar magnitude throughout the period. These effects change over time, but in a manner that defies simple characterization as beneficial or detrimental to women. Relative to men, women gained greater access to jobs; however, female disadvantage in the quality of new jobs widened.

Gender, Labor Market Outcomes and Post-Socialist Transition: The Soviet Legacy and Market Reforms

Soviet women never reached earnings parity with men, despite the egalitarian claims of socialism. The Soviet-era gender wage gap was comparable to levels found in advanced capitalist societies. . . . Official Soviet ideals and chronic labor shortages pushed women into the labor force. State-sponsored childcare and maternity leaves helped women participate in the labor market at nearly the same rate as men. The centralized system for determining wages left managers little leeway to differentially allocate pay, making sex segregation by occupation and economic branch the primary sources of observed wage differentials. On average women earned about 70 percent of what men did, but the narrow Soviet wage distribution meant a lower gender gap in absolute wages than in societies with wider distributions. . . .

In January 1992 the new Russian government introduced sweeping market reforms. They removed most controls on prices, wages, trade and currency exchange (exposing Russian firms to foreign competition), eliminated planning and mandatory state orders, curtailed enterprise subsidies, removed restrictions on private ownership of productive assets, and privatized small firms. Mass privatization of medium and large state firms started in 1993.

Russia's reformers hoped competitive pressures would compel managers to respond to market signals by improving efficiency and re-structuring their product lines and work-forces. Enterprises would be divested of their social distribution functions and transformed into profit-making, competitive entities. Unemployment would increase, as inefficient enterprises closed and successful enterprises shed excess labor. In fact, the reforms, in combination with fluctuating monetary policies and prior structural conditions, set off hyperinflation, steep declines in output and real wages, steady growth in unemployment, and a sharp rise in inequality until growth resumed after 1998. . . .

"We doubt that Russian employers lost their taste for discrimination against women; instead, they eventually found it too costly to satisfy."

Discussion

. . . At the end of the Soviet era, women faced disadvantages in rates of layoff, employment entry, and among those without a college education, inter-firm job changes. Following market reforms, the first two disadvantages declined and even reversed. By 1997 men had substantially higher layoff rates than women, and unemployed women found work faster than unemployed men. Improving opportunities for female employment help explain growing gender parity in voluntary employment exit rates. As women grew more confident that they could find future employment, they were less afraid to quit their jobs. Women's access to employment increased relative to men's during Russia's post-socialist transition period. These findings contradict claims . . . that women have been overrepresented among the new unemployed in Russia.

At the same time, the gender gap in the quality of new jobs has remained stable or widened. With one exception— access to jobs in new private firms—Russian women have been increasingly excluded from high-quality jobs and channeled into low-quality jobs. Even as the labor market has given women more opportunities for employment, it has become more segmented by gender in ways that increase women's economic disadvantages.

How can market reforms both increase women's relative access to employment and channel them away from high-quality jobs toward low-quality jobs? We see both trends as related to one another and to the process of post-socialist transition. The combined forces of market competition and lower female wages underlie expanded female access to employment. Early in the transition, employers who wished to discriminate against women could do so after the state withdrew supports for female employment. Initially they perceived few economic incentives not to discriminate, due to lack of familiarity with market institutions and uncertainty as to how long market reforms would last. But as the transition progressed, they learned that they had to cut labor costs without sacrificing productivity to compete with domestic and foreign firms. Meanwhile, they realized that women offer a better bargain in productivity per unit cost. Prior gender discrimination implies that remaining female employees were more productive on average than the remaining male employees. Also, female wages were lower, and increasingly so, for comparable work. Eventually the forces of market competition and labor market gender segmentation combined to provide strong incentives for hiring and retaining female rather than male employees. We doubt that Russian employers lost their taste for discrimination against women; instead, they eventually found it too costly to satisfy.

Apart from the trends we have identified, three other findings are consistent with this interpretation. First, between January 1991 and January 1998 the average occupational percent female increased for both men and women by 3 to 4 percentage points. This implies that employers favored hiring people for jobs in female-dominated occupations. Presumably, they were motivated by the lower wages of such occupations: the correlation between the mean logged earnings and the percent female in an occupation is -. 54. Russian employers facing competitive pressure could cut costs by shifting the balance of their workforces toward feminized occupations, making whatever adjustments necessary in their product lines and operations. Expanding female-dominated occupations should increase female employment opportunities.

Second, early in the transition female job changers with college degrees were more likely than equivalent males to land in new private firms. In contrast to privatized firms, the managers and owners of new private firms had to be concerned with competition and cost-cutting from the outset. The early timing of their preference for highly qualified females over highly qualified males confirms our interpretation that market pressures (combined with lower female wages) enhance female access to employment.

Third, growing female disadvantage in the quality of new jobs provides evidence for the second part of the equation: female wages have decreased (lowering the relative cost of female labor) due to gender segmentation of the labor market. In turn, the decrease in women's wages stems proximately from their greater propensity to take jobs in low-wage industries, lower-paying occupations and the state sector, as well as their lower propensity to take jobs in high-wage branches and (net of control variables) better-paying occupations. Thus, increasing female disadvantage in the quality of new jobs complements women's improving access to employment in post-socialist Russia. As the average quality of women's jobs declines, so do women's wages, making them more attractive to employers.

Why are Russian women more likely to take poorer quality jobs? They must have, on average, lower reservation wages than Russian men. Female-headed households are especially poor, so female heads are desperate to accept any job that is

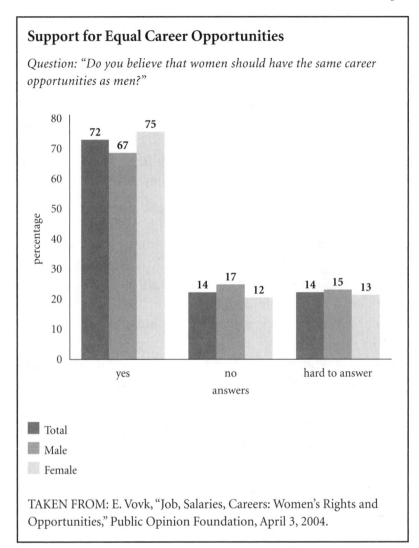

Support for Equal Career Opportunities

Question: "Do you believe that women should have the same career opportunities as men?"

TAKEN FROM: E. Vovk, "Job, Salaries, Careers: Women's Rights and Opportunities," Public Opinion Foundation, April 3, 2004.

available. In dual-headed households, women often have secondary earner status. The gender gap in reservation wages may have increased during the economic crisis of the 1990s, which has put greater pressure on the budgets of all types of households. Gender norms inherited from the Soviet era could make lower female wages self-reproducing by reducing women's expectations, leading them to accept jobs men would not.

[One critic argues], based on interviews, that the Soviet gender order encouraged women to work, but also to put their families first and accept secondary status at work as natural. Still guided by such norms, when women look for work they emphasize stability of income rather than to the level of pay or status. In contrast, men define their status—as in Soviet times—through their work, so they prioritize pay and status over providing for their families. [The] female interviewees saw little chance for improving their job positions, while the men were more optimistic.

Other cultural factors—e. g., sex-stereotyping of certain occupations, branches of the economy and types of work—could also play a role. Such factors might also account for the lower propensity of women to enter better-paying occupations (which tend to be male dominated) and high-wage branches. Of course, employers could discriminate. Our data do not contain the information needed to rigorously test these alternative explanations. But whatever the explanation, our results clearly show growing female disadvantage in the quality of new jobs, which (somewhat ironically) makes women more attractive employees in an increasingly competitive context by driving down their average wages.

". . . when women look for work they emphasize stability of income rather than to the level of pay or status. In contrast, men define their status—as in Soviet times—through their work. . . ."

The gender gap in earnings cannot be attributed to changes in the overall wage distribution, as some have argued. . . . Gender affects movements in and out of employment, job mobility and the quality of the new jobs that result from job mobility, all of which affect wages. The pattern whereby Russian women have become more likely than men to be employed, but also to be employed in poorer quality jobs, could account for growth in the gender wage gap, particularly if men at the bottom of the earnings distribution are more likely to be unemployed (and hence have no observed wages).

The patterns we identify in Russia may not hold true for other former socialist countries. The impact of market transition on inequality generally depends on the particular policies by which reforms are implemented, pre-existing structural conditions and the precise institutional trajectories in a given country.... Prior gender differences in human capital and structural location, as well as cultural and political factors such as the prevalence of patriarchal attitudes and the strength of feminist movements, might also shape how markets affect gender inequality. Only rigorous cross-national comparisons can reveal whether there are common patterns of dynamic gender effects in post-socialist labor markets. But such comparisons require more systematic empirical work on individual countries. Our study of Russia shows that a dynamic approach to modeling the effects of gender on movements in and out of employment, job mobility and the quality of new jobs can yield unique insights into the connection between gender inequality and market reforms.

One important task for future research on gender differences in the Russian labor market will be to expand the time frame of analysis. Since 1998, the Russian economy has improved steadily, and market institutions have established firmer roots compared to the mid 1990s. Perhaps a different gender dynamic has emerged in the context of improving employment and wages. A second key task will be to incorporate measures (lacking in our data) of marital status, household size and household structure, to explicitly test whether the effects of gender on labor market outcomes vary by family situation....

South Africa Offers Women Programs for Economic Empowerment

Elizabeth Thabethe

The South African government has implemented several programs to encourage and support women-owned businesses, reports Elizabeth Thabethe in the following viewpoint. They include a women entrepreneurs' fund, a program for women to accelerate their economic empowerment by using technology-based solutions, and a program designed to bridge the gap between black and white economic growth left by apartheid. Thabethe states that South Africa needs to promote its status as host of the 2010 World Cup sporting event to generate greater and more widespread economic activity. Thabethe is deputy minister of trade and industry for the South African government.

As you read, consider the following questions:

1. How many years does Elizabeth Thabethe say it took for the women in the 1956 women's march to achieve their political freedom?

2. According to the viewpoint, what is the monetary range of loans to be provided by the Industrial Development Corporation?

Elizabeth Thabethe, "Keynote Address Delivered by Deputy Minister of Trade and Industry Ms. Elizabeth Thabethe During the Launch of the South African Owner Drivers Empowerment Federation Women in Transport Structure," South African Government Information, July 20, 2007. Reproduced by permission.

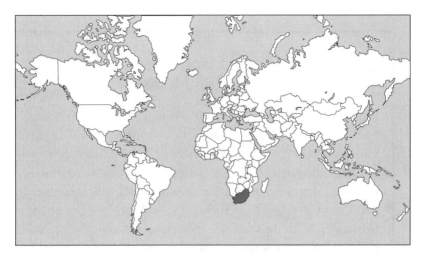

3. What does the acronym TWIB stand for and what is its purpose?

Getting started in any business is not an easy task; getting into "predominantly male" dominated business is even more so. I therefore wish to wish the organisation every success with this launch.

It gives me great pleasure to address you here today on this very relevant topic of women's economic empowerment. It is heartening to note that the organisers did not wait for August [2007], the much celebrated national Women's Month, to address this matter. It took 38 years for the women of the 1956 Women's March to achieve their political freedom. We would be doing a disservice to their proud legacy if we took the same number of years for women to achieve their economic freedom.

Access to finance and business opportunities for women seems to be a universal problem, judging from issues raised by women at conferences I have attended since becoming Deputy Minister of Trade and Industry. The challenges are daunting but not insurmountable. In our favour as South African women is the unwavering support from the presidency, where

Japan's Equal Employment Reform Supports Working Mothers

When Japan passed its Equal Employment Opportunity Law (EEOL) in 1985, public support for women's rights was very low. For example, only 18.1 percent of Japanese citizens thought it was a good idea for women to continue to work after having children.... By 2005, that number had risen to 40.4 percent in support of mothers working.... Along with the policy and social attitudinal changes, issues in work and family emerged and developed in post-EEOL Japan, ... [which] has been increasingly affected by globalization. Topics such as women's employment rights and men's family involvement were not particularly popular topics for discussion in the national politics and media before the legal reform. Today, however, the national media intensively cover issues such as problems of women leaving ... work, due to the difficulty of taking family leave or sexual harassment at work. Similarly, men's challenges at work, such as the extremely low rates of men's family leave use, are also becoming popular issues for discussion. These social changes in the Japanese perspectives illuminate the importance of EEOL reforms, which affected social processes and institutional structures, raising issues in family and work.

Chika Shinohara,
"Transforming Law and Social Consciousness in Japan:
Perspectives on Contemporary Issues in Family and Work,"
Department of Sociology, University of Minnesota,
January 17, 2007, p. 3.

President [Thabo] Mbeki and Deputy President [Phumzile] Mlambo-Ngcuka have shown their commitment to the cause of women.

The Department Is Dedicated to Women's Economic Empowerment

As one of the two Deputy Ministers of Trade and Industry it is my responsibility to attend to matters of women's economic empowerment as one of the tasks delegated to me. To indicate the importance of this issue we have a dedicated unit responsible for gender and women's empowerment in the Department of Trade and Industry [DTI]. This unit is one of the programmes established by the current Deputy President while she was still the Deputy Minister of Trade and Industry!

Accelerated and shared growth means ensuring an equitable share of our economy between men and women. The Department of Trade and Industry has dedicated itself to continue its efforts to increase the participation of women in the South African economy through further implementation of the Strategic Framework on Gender and Women's Economic Empowerment. The framework is a major intervention led by the DTI aimed at addressing the market failures of economic policies and programmes in addressing gender equity in South Africa. It is primarily aimed at fast-tracking women's economic empowerment while ensuring that the issue is institutionalised as a critical aspect of government's national economic agenda. The strategy is further aimed at ensuring that sufficient well-budgeted resources are made available for programmes relevant to women empowerment.

One of the major interventions proposed by the strategy is the establishment of the South African Women's Entrepreneurs Fund. The fund is to be launched during this financial year [2007–08] and will provide loans and business support to develop profitable women-owned enterprises. A decision has been made to appoint the Industrial Development Corporation (IDC) as the institution to administer this fund. The fund is geared toward addressing the funding needs of women-owned enterprises with loans ranging from R[rand; South African currency]10 00 to R250 000 as one category and loans from R250 000 to R1 million as another. The unique selling point of this fund will be to provide these enterprises with special procurement or tender loans to be able to render relevant services after being awarded a tender deal.

"Accelerated and shared growth means ensuring an equitable share of our economy between men and women."

SAWEN Plays an Important Role

The further strengthening of South African Women Entrepreneurs' Network (SAWEN) has also been identified as a major intervention of the strategic framework. SAWEN has created a solid foundation in establishing a national forum for the engagement of women entrepreneurs. There is absolutely no doubt that SAWEN has become the beacon of hope for South African women entrepreneurs who continue to find it difficult to access the DTI independently. Moreover, SAWEN has continued [to] be a viable strategic partner of provincial economic departments in delivering some of their programmes for women. This has led to some of the provinces cosponsoring the establishment of provincial offices.

During this financial year [2007–08], the DTI will review the status of SAWEN. This will include embarking on a process of ensuring that SAWEN becomes one of the DTI-listed entities. The DTI recognises the important role that SAWEN plays as a broker between DTI delivery agencies and women entrepreneurs. The review will look at the role that SAWEN plays and how it can be enhanced to strengthen the participation of women in the economy.

Other Programs Help Disadvantaged Sectors

We also have the Technology for Women in Business [TWIB] programme, an initiative of the DTI. More commonly know as TWIB its mandate is to accelerate women's economic empowerment and women-owned entrepreneurial development through the facilitation of scientific and technology-based business applications and systems. There is an annual competition open to solely/majority women-owned businesses who have managed to bridge the technological divide in the running of their enterprises.

To address the legacy of underdevelopment left by apartheid it has been necessary for government to implement vigorous programmes that will start to assist in bridging the divide between the first and second economy. In this respect Broad Based Black Economic Empowerment (BBBEE) has been one of the tools decided upon to start fixing this skewed economic growth. As the Department of Trade and Industry, we have released the BBBEE Codes of Good Practice in our concerted effort to ensure that the historically disadvantaged sectors of our communities now also have an opportunity to participate in economic activities.

There is no doubt in everyone's mind that small, medium and micro enterprises (SMMEs) will play a critical role in our efforts to broaden the base of our economic participation. In an endeavour to integrate BBBEE and SMME development, the Codes of Good Practice will address the SMME. While the codes try to protect enterprises, particularly those that are very small and micro, we also seek to ensure that those within the threshold of compliance benefit through a number of measures encapsulated in the principles of Black Economic Empowerment (BEE).

"To address the legacy of underdevelopment left by apartheid it has been necessary for government to implement vigorous programmes that will start to assist in bridging the divide between the first and second economy."

There might be an inverse relation between the requirements for BBBEE compliance by enterprises suppliers and

SMMEs; however family businesses and/or SMMEs are recognised and acknowledged as an integral part of the South African economy, among others, because of the very high leverage factor this sector has on job creation. In this regard, the Department of Trade and Industry will do everything in its power to protect, grow and develop this sector. The department will guide the private sector SMME-implementation of the broad-based BEE Codes of Good Practice, with particular reference here to the enterprise development aspects of the code. In this respect, the BBBEE codes will be an important source of demand for emerging small enterprises and will be a driver of transformation in our economy.

Of course no program is without its loopholes and challenges and I want to urge businesswomen here today to be wary of 'fronting'. Get what is due to you from deals you enter into in partnerships offered to you.

Incentive Programs Are Available to Small and Big Businesses

The Department of Trade and Industry has numerous incentive schemes and nonfinancial support services run by the various DTI agencies that can be accessed by SMMEs and also big business. Amongst these are:

- South African Micro-Finance Apex Fund (SAMAF), Apex Fund

- Industrial Development Corporation (IDC)

- National Empowerment Fund (NEF)

- Khula

- Small Enterprise Development Agency (SEDA).

Ladies and gentlemen, South Africa is alive with possibilities, the most significant event to come to our country being the World Cup in 2010; is this not a vote of confidence in our ability as a country to host the second biggest world sporting event? Yet, I find that this confidence has not rubbed off on us as South Africans. Landing at our international airports there is very little sign of this momentous event coming to our country. We should be telling the world that we were chosen, we are good enough, and we are capable! Where are the T-shirts, caps and flags or the vuvuzelas saying, "World Cup 2010 Proudly South African", where are the signs on our taxis, busses and trucks saying this?

We are looking at how our businesses, especially SMMEs can benefit. How we can ensure strong and meaningful BEE participation, achieve greater geographic spread of economic activity and ensure an outcome of a sustainable legacy from the event.

Notwithstanding the challenges, there is institutional support and more importantly, political support to assist you to become successful entrepreneurs. Where we are failing in our duty to you, let us know. We have a historical obligation to see you succeed, the 20,000 women in the 1956 march through that singular action, demands that we meet that obligation. The future direction for developing women entrepreneurs is indeed firmly rooted in the past!

Thai Women Are Increasingly Affected by the Economic Downturn

Lynette Lee Corporal

In the following viewpoint, Lynette Lee Corporal states that the worldwide economic downturn is hitting Thai women particularly hard since they are in jobs that are the first to be cut as overseas factories close and cut back. The government is trying to implement programs to ease the burden, she asserts, but citizens wonder where the money will come from in such a tight economy. Critics say the problems warrant long-term solutions that redefine and address the real roots of poverty. Asia Media Forum is a network of journalists in Asia who share insights about the media and their profession, stories, and information about issues in the region including democracy, development, and human rights. Corporal is a projects editor for the Inter Press Service, Asia-Pacific. She has fourteen years of experience in the media industry.

As you read, consider the following questions:

1. In Lynette Lee Corporal's estimation, what is Benjawan Marongthong's monthly household income in U.S. dollars?

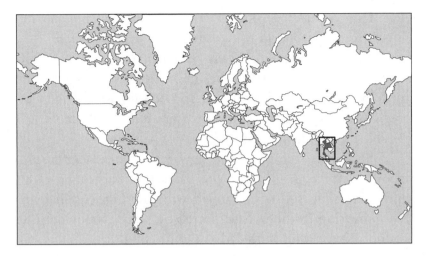

2. According to the International Labour Organization, what was the percentage increase in the unemployment rate for women workers in Southeast Asia in 2008?

3. How many job vacancies were there in Thailand at the time this viewpoint was written?

"Please help me find a way to have some money for milk," pleaded Benjawan Marongthong, mother of two young boys and former worker in a garments factory.

Laid off two years ago and unable to find work at a time when the ranks of the unemployed are swelling as a result of the global economic downturn, Benjawan is almost at the end of her rope.

With her husband the only breadwinner in her family, she has to make the most of the household's monthly income of 9,000 baht (247 US dollars). "I'd like the government to at least help reduce the social security contribution of 400 baht (11 dollars) we are required to pay every month," she said. She was referring to the workers' share of social security.

Speaking at a workshop on the 'Impact of the Economic Crisis on Women Workers,' organised by the Friedrich Ebert Foundation and the Women Workers' Unity Group (WWUG), here Thursday [April 2009], Benjawan's plight is not too different from that of a growing number of Thai workers.

While many had to closely watch their expenses before, they are now finding themselves in dire straits as factories, hit by falling overseas orders in Asia and beyond, are closing, cutting work hours or wages. Women are among the most vulnerable groups in this crisis.

"While it is true that women were able to enter the Thai labour sector better than in the past, their bargaining rights and overall job security, coupled with the burdens of being the family breadwinner, have decreased," Thai labour minister Paitoon Kaewthong conceded at the meeting.

Women Are More Susceptible to Job Cuts

"The majority of women workers are becoming disproportionately susceptible to job cuts and are more likely to be harder hit by rising unemployment," added Alice Chang, labour director of Union Network International (UNI) Global Union - Asia and the Pacific Region, a network of trade unions totaling two million workers.

Even in the most optimistic of scenarios, Chang said that the number of unemployed Thai women is expected to increase by 144 percent this year.

Historically, Thailand has had much lower unemployment rates than neigbours like the Philippines, for instance, but the problems are no less real in this Southeast Asian country.

Thailand's unemployment rate stood at 1.4 percent in 2008, or about 530,000 people. While this was much lower than the 5.7 percent average of other Southeast Asian countries, there are worrisome signs for Thailand. For instance, the National Statistics Office said the poverty rate for 2008 reached 8.9 percent, up from 8.5 in 2007—the first increase since 2000.

The National Economic and Social Development Board, the state planning agency, reported that the country's unemployment rate is expected to rise to 2.5 percent in 2009. This means that more than 900,000 out of a national labour force of 37.6 million workers could be jobless this year [2006]. In 1998, during Thailand's worst economic crisis, the unemployment rate hit 4.4 percent.

"Thailand's unemployment rate stood at 1.4 percent in 2008, or about 530,000 people."

The Thai government has been trying to create economic stimulus packages to help stem the unemployment tide, including a recent decision to give employees who earn less than 15,000 baht (411.78 dollars) a month, a one-time assistance package of 2,000 baht (55 dollars).

Chang noted, however, that "none of these plans have any specific measures for women workers".

A report released March 5 [2006] by the International Labour Organization echoes the same concerns for women workers during hard times. The unemployment rate in 2008 for women workers in Southeast Asia was 6 percent, up from 5.8 percent in 2007.

In South Asia, the unemployment rates stayed at 6 percent in both years. For this year, the report *Global Employment Trends for Women 2009* says female unemployment rates in Southeast Asia and the Pacific could range from 6.5 to 6.8 percent (8 million women) and from 6 to 6.8 percent (11 to 13 million people) in South Asia.

Women Do Not Have a Strong Social Safety Net

Informal workers, who include many women, are also feeling the pinch because they have fewer social safety nets than those in the formal sector. According to the Bangkok-based United

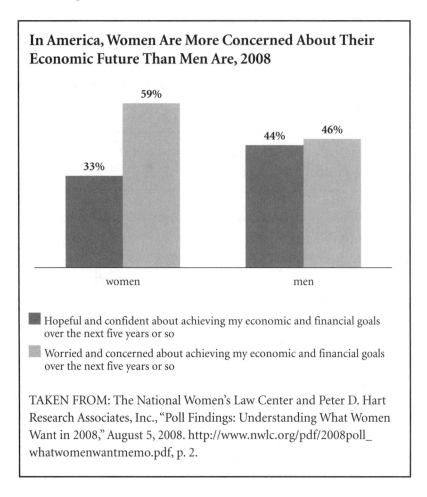

In America, Women Are More Concerned About Their Economic Future Than Men Are, 2008

- Hopeful and confident about achieving my economic and financial goals over the next five years or so
- Worried and concerned about achieving my economic and financial goals over the next five years or so

TAKEN FROM: The National Women's Law Center and Peter D. Hart Research Associates, Inc., "Poll Findings: Understanding What Women Want in 2008," August 5, 2008. http://www.nwlc.org/pdf/2008poll_whatwomenwantmemo.pdf, p. 2.

Nations Economic and Social Commission for Asia and the Pacific [ESCAP], 65 percent of working women in the region are in the informal sector, which means they work as contractual or casual workers and are not entitled to full workers' benefits.

In a set of proposals presented to the workshop participants, the 46 organisations under the Women Workers' Unity Group asked the government to set up support funds for laid-off workers, promote job-training skills for workers in small and medium enterprises, provide employment and reduce social security contributions.

Minister Paitoon maintained that the Thai government is closely monitoring the number of workers being let go and taking some measures to help ease the unemployed workers' burden.

"Informal workers, who include many women, are . . . feeling the pinch because they have fewer social safety nets than those in the formal sector."

On Jan. 7 [2006], the ministry of labour announced the disbursement of 10 billion baht (277 million dollars) to help ease unemployment woes. Paitoon was quoted in newspaper reports as saying that the budget would be spent on "professional training activities for about 500,000 jobless employees" who would also be given an allowance of about 200 baht (five dollars) per day.

"Already, five million workers have indicated interest about this grant," he said.

But Chang has reservations about workers demanding that "government give us more money". "Where will this money come from? If income drops and tax from workers drops, how is the government going to get money? What you want is not to get money, but get employed back."

According to the minister, there are about 100,000 job vacancies at present and the labour ministry is organising another job fair on Mar. 20 and 21 [2006] in the Thai capital.

"If there aren't enough job vacancies, then we might propose that we reduce the number of jobs for migrant workers and give these posts to Thais. Of course, we will give the migrant workers assistance and compensation as well," he added.

Chang sees the minister's proposal as problematic. "The minister's proposal to kick out migrant workers and give the jobs to Thais will not work. You have to remember that there are many Thai migrant workers in other countries as well. If you start kicking migrant workers out, then other countries might also start kicking out Thai workers. Employment rights for foreign workers must be protected as well," said Chang, a specialist on women's issues.

Problems Need Long-Term Solutions

For Voravidh Charoenloet of Chiang Mai University, the problem should be addressed with long-term solutions, instead of measures like the 55-dollar assistance. "The 2007 economic crisis won't end within two years because this is a global issue we're facing here," he said.

It is also not enough telling the unemployed to go back to the countryside and find work there. To address the problem, he said, one must look at deeper issues of income gaps and land reform.

Echoing the professor's sentiments, parliamentarian and human rights activist Rachdaporn Kaewsanit said that Thailand must adopt measures that will support the agricultural industry "if you talk about workers going back to their hometowns for good".

"We need to redefine poverty—is it the lack of money or the lack of food? We need to have a change in attitude," she explained.

Periodical Bibliography

The following articles have been selected to supplement the diverse views presented in this chapter.

Haifa Fahoum Al Kaylani	"Women Are Agents of Change," Common Ground News Service, March 4, 2008. www.commongroundnews.org.
Susan M. Andersen and Christina S. Kooij	"Adult Literacy Education and Human Rights: A View from Afghanistan," *Globalisation, Societies and Education*, November 2007.
Duncan Hewitt	"China's Women Fight for Their Rights," *Newsweek*, August 17, 2009.
Mutsuko Murakami	"Rights-Japan: Women Talk: 'We Want Greater Gender Equality,'" Inter Press Service, September 29, 2009. http://ipsnews.net.
Andrew Purvis	"Why Merkel Is Not Enough," *Time Europe*, January 22, 2006.
Yigal Schleifer	"Rural Women's Crafts Reaching Global Markets," Women's eNews, August 21, 2005. www.womensenews.org.
Spiegel Online International	"Gender and Climate Change: Poor Women Bear Brunt of Global Warming," November 20, 2009. www.speigel.de.
Haifa Zangana	"Women and Learning in the Iraqi War Zone," *International Journal of Lifelong Education*, March 2008.

For Further Discussion

Chapter 1

1. Marwaan Macan-Markar asserts that women and men political prisoners in Burma are abused. What does Macan-Markar have to say about the current political climate in Burma?

2. Stephanie Nieuwoudt states that increasing the number of women eligible to vote in South Africa might actually be a disservice to increasing women's roles in local government. The International Institute for Communication and Development is a proponent of increasing indigenous women's leadership roles in government. Why do the two viewpoints differ in their approach to expanding women's roles in governing their own region?

Chapter 2

1. Alvaro Serrano reports that the Islamic Republic of Iran has successfully implemented family planning policies that do not violate the tenets of Islam. Dewanti Lakhsmi Sari believes that Islam recognizes that male-female relationships can be defined within a modern context but still remain true to Islamic law. What are the differences and similarities in how Islam's beliefs are described in the two viewpoints? Are there any inconsistencies between the viewpoints expressed by Serrano and Sari?

Chapter 3

1. Barbara Hans describes honor killings and repercussions of the act against an Afghan girl living in Germany. Do you think the author portrays the issue objectively as a journalist or as an advocate for one side of the issue?

What information in the viewpoint illuminates Hans's approach to the subject matter? How does the information in Hans's viewpoint align with the viewpoint expressed in Esfandiari's description of changes in Afghanistan's laws?

2. Sybil Sheridan recounts the kinds of women and areas of women's lives that contibuted to the prayers in the Yiddish tehinnot. Are there non-Jewish traditions of women's prayer books?

Chapter 4

1. Susan Diduk provides a detailed picture of the protest marches of farm women in Cameroon. What does Diduk say about the effectiveness of the women's style of protest?

2. Elizabeth Thabethe promotes the view that the South African government is actively supporting programs to assist women-owned businesses. What are the programs to assist women? What is the first and second economy? Where do women fit in this economic structure?

Organizations to Contact

The editors have compiled the following list of organizations concerned with the issues debated in this book. The descriptions are derived from materials provided by the organizations. All have publications or information available for interested readers. The list was compiled on the date of publication of the present volume; names, addresses, phone and fax numbers, and e-mail and Internet addresses may change. Be aware that many organizations take several weeks or longer to respond to inquiries, so allow as much time as possible.

Asian Indigenous Women's Network (AIWN)
1 Roman Ayson Road, Baguio City   2600
   Philippines
(63) 74-4447703 • fax: (63) 74-4439459
Web site: www.asianindigenouswomen.org

The Asian Indigenous Women's Network (AIWN) supports, sustains, and helps consolidate various efforts of indigenous women in Asia. It empowers indigenous women by helping them become aware of their rights as women and as indigenous peoples and helps them develop their own organizations and structures for empowerment. The organization publishes *AIWN Magazine* and has conducted two Asian Indigenous Women's Conferences.

Women in Islam
PO Box 814, Lincolnton Station, New York, NY   10037-0814
(212) 576-8875 • fax: (212) 491-9185
e-mail: womeninislam@usa.net
Web site: www.womeninislam.org

Women in Islam is an organization of professional and social activist Muslim women dedicated to the empowerment of women through the knowledge and practice of Islam. Members provide a forum for action to help improve the quality of life for Muslim women at home and abroad. Their objective is to address issues pertinent to Muslim communities worldwide and build understanding across cultural boundaries in the interest of global social justice. The organization sponsors programs such as Charting Our Own Course: Celebrating Women's History Month and lectures on human rights and social justice.

Women's Action for New Directions (WAND)

691 Massachusetts Avenue, Arlington, MA   02476
(781) 643-6740 • fax: (781) 643-6744
e-mail: peace@wand.org
Web site: www.wand.org

Women's Action for New Directions (WAND) empowers women to act politically to reduce violence and militarism, and redirect excessive military resources toward unmet human and environmental needs. WAND's program Students Take Action for New Directions (STAND) empowers young women to act politically to promote peace, equality, and progressive social change. The organization's publications include *Can We Clear the Nuclear Shadow? A Moment for Hope* and *Federal Budget Study Guide.*

Women's Global Network for Reproductive Rights (WGNRR)

Coordination Office, 13 Dao Street, Project 3
Barangay Quirino 3-A, Quezon City   1102
    Philippines
(63) 2-913-6708 • fax: (63) 2-911-8293
e-mail: office@wgnrr.org
Web site: www.wgnrr.org

Women's Global Network for Reproductive Rights (WGNRR) is a network of two thousand autonomous organizations and individuals from 157 countries. Since 1984, WGNRR has worked to improve and support reproductive and sexual health rights for women. The organization publishes a newsletter and reports.

Women's Legal Education and Action Fund (LEAF)

60 St. Clair Avenue E, Suite 703

Toronto, Ontario   M4T 1N5
  Canada

(416) 595-7170 • fax: (416) 595-7191

e-mail: info@leaf.ca

Web site: www.leaf.ca

Women's Legal Education and Action Fund (LEAF) is a national charitable organization that works toward ensuring the law guarantees substantive equality for all women in Canada. It ensures that the rights of women and girls in Canada are upheld in the country's courts, human rights commissions, and government agencies. It also reveals how factors such as race, class, Aboriginal status, sexual orientation, ability, and religion compound discrimination against women. LEAF publishes reports including *Equality Rights in Family Law: Spousal and Child Support* and *Making Equality Rights Real: Securing Substantive Equality Under the Charter.*

Women'sNet

PO Box 62577, Marshalltown   2107
  South Africa

(27) 11-429-0000 • fax: (27) 11-838-9871

e-mail: women@womensnet.org.za

Web site: www.womensnet.org.za

Women'sNet is a feminist organization that works to advance gender equality and justice in South Africa using information and communication technologies (ICTs). It provides training and facilitates content dissemination and creation that support women, girls, organizations, and networks to take control of their own content and ICT use. It helps women find people, issues, resources, and tools needed for social activism. Women'sNet publishes the *Intersection* newsletter and reports such as *Women's Rights: Looking Back or Moving Forward?*

WomenWatch
Inter-Agency Network on Women and Gender Equality
2 United Nations Plaza, 12th floor, New York, NY 10017
(212) 963-4475
e-mail: womenwatch@un.org
We site: www.un.org/womenwatch

WomenWatch is the central gateway to information and resources on the promotion of gender equality and the empowerment of women throughout the United Nations system. WomenWatch is an initiative of the Inter-Agency Network on Women and Gender Equality, which publishes numerous reports including *State of World Population 2009*, *Women and Health: Today's Evidence, Tomorrow's Agenda*, and *2009 World Survey on the Role of Women in Development*.

Bibliography of Books

Nitza Berkovitch   *From Motherhood to Citizenship: Women's Rights and International Organizations.* Baltimore, MD: Johns Hopkins University Press, 1999.

Ester Boserup   *Woman's Role in Economic Development.* London: Earthscan, 2007.

Shawn Meghan Burn   *Women Across Cultures: A Global Perspective.* New York: McGraw-Hill, 2005.

Asghar Ali Engineer   *The Rights of Women in Islam.* Elgin, IL: New Dawn Press, 2004.

V.S. Ganesamurthy, ed.   *Empowerment of Women in India: Social, Economic, and Political.* New Delhi: New Century Publications, 2008.

Catharine A. MacKinnon   *Are Women Human? And Other International Dialogues.* Cambridge, MA: Belknap Press of Harvard University Press, 2006.

Laura Reichenbach and Mindy Jane Roseman, eds.   *Reproductive Health and Human Rights: The Way Forward.* Philadelphia: University of Pennsylvania Press, 2009.

Deborah L. Rhode and Carol Sanger   *Gender and Rights.* Burlington, VT: Ashgate, 2005.

Sandy Ruxton, ed.   *Gender Equality and Men: Learning from Practice.* Oxford: Oxfam Publishing, 2004.

Faegheh Shirazi   *Velvet Jihad: Muslim Women's Quiet Resistance to Islamic Fundamentalism.* Gainesville, FL: University Press of Florida, 2009.

Jael Silliman, Marlene Gerber Fried, Loretta Ross, and Elena R. Gutiérrez   *Undivided Rights: Women of Color Organize for Reproductive Justice.* Cambridge, MA: South End Press, 2004.

Sharon Smith   *Women and Socialism: Essays on Women's Liberation.* Chicago, IL: Haymarket Books, 2005.

United Nations Division for the Advancement of Women   *Ending Violence Against Women: From Words to Action.* New York: United Nations, 2006.

Christien L. van den Anker and Jeroen Doomernik, eds.   *Trafficking and Women's Rights.* New York: Palgrave Macmillan, 2006.

Lynn Welchman, ed.   *Women's Rights and Islamic Family Law: Perspectives on Reform.* London: Zed Books, 2004.

Adrien Katherine Wing, ed.   *Global Critical Race Feminism: An International Reader.* New York: New York University Press, 2000.

Index

Geographic headings and page numbers in **boldface** refer to viewpoints about that country or region.